The Soul's Power

The Soul's Power

A Memoir of the Spirit through the Journey of MS

Maureen Philpott Napier

iUniverse, Inc.
New York   Bloomington

The Soul's Power
A Memoir of the Spirit through the Journey of MS

iUniverse books may be ordered through booksellers or by contacting:

iUniverse
1663 Liberty Drive
Bloomington, IN 47403
www.iuniverse.com
1-800-Authors (1-800-288-4677)

ISBN: 978-1-4401-9368-2 (pbk)
ISBN: 978-1-4401-9370-5 (cloth)
ISBN: 978-1-4401-9369-9 (ebook)

Library of Congress Control Number: 2009913863

Printed in the United States of America

iUniverse rev. date: 12/18/2009

Soul's Walk

Are the steps of one's journey
Taken by the steps that we walk
Or by the steps one's heart, one's soul
Without walking at all

Maureen Philpott Napier
2005

In loving memory of my grandparents,
Mary and John Hanlon of St. Boswells, Scotland
~Love is a fragrant rose in continual bloom~
—Maureen Philpott Napier

And also to all heroes who walk their lives with MS, for never giving up and always, no matter how dark their days, finding the light within themselves that tells the world,
~I will live well with MS~
—Maureen Philpott Napier

A portion of the proceeds of this book will be donated to the MS Society
~Together we can find the cure~
—Maureen Philpott Napier

CONTENTS

The Road through Disease

I see the mountain before me
So tall and elusive
Its strength dominates
And challenges all that come near
It beckons thy soul
To be one with the stone
For in being as One
The elusive mountain
Is a challenge no more

Maureen Philpott Napier
March 30, 2006

Introduction

This story is my unique journey and the account of my life after suffering a paralyzing multiple sclerosis (MS) attack on March 26, 2006. On that day, a fundamental *life* change left me no choice but to battle the relentless onslaught of progressive damage from a neurological disease. A chronicled journey of the stark, naked truth of the kinds of despair, reflection, triumph, and inspiration living with MS can bring. Writing it became a release of what surged through my soul as I continued to seek healing and a deeper understanding within myself, of myself. The words written within these pages were not only the instrument of my surrender but also the instrument of my acceptance and thus transcendence of this life's limits living with MS. At times, this journey may grip your heart, but it's my hope that it will also reveal to you the power and the wisdom within your own soul. To allow our true inner beauty to be seen, no matter our challenges ... To always sense the Divine light within us, even if only a flicker, no matter how dark and deep our sorrows may be ... these are the messages I want to convey. There is "a knowing" within that eased my pain, lifted my despair, and ultimately healed my heart and soul. I wish to pass this "knowing" on to you.

As you read this book, we will traverse the MS path together, allowing all that surfaces to float away. It is my desire that you will not only feel release from suffering, but also be inspired to live well, no matter the confines MS, or any other disease, or illness, may cause you.

Together, we will face the challenges, sorrows, and darkness and let go of the fear, feeling love and strengthening the Divine light within us all. *The Soul's Power* has been my passion, the very steps my spirit walked, the Divine energy within me that propelled my soul to always take a step forwards, no matter how many times I fell. To continue to nourish, heal, and awaken the spirit that I am, to intimately know the power, courage and wisdom within my own soul: This is my new life.

In the hospital, as I lay partially paralyzed and confined to a stretcher, there was actually two independent problems that helped confuse the ER staff as they tried to navigate through my symptoms. First, I was suffering from a severe migraine attack on the right side of my head as usual; it was exploding like an erupting volcano. The head pain would, within hours, spread to encompass my whole head, both left and right hemispheres of the brain. Light and noise seemed to magnify and prolong the excruciating head pain. Second, I had no regular feeling, only a numbing or freezing effect from my neck to toes on the right side of my body. Eventually I would have no feeling on that side at all, except when sharp electrical pains periodically shot down the right side of my body as my leg and arm went into spasms. The pain was unbearable. But it wasn't all. There was also a deep confusion, an *emptiness of thoughts*, an inability to remember who I was or understand what was happening to me. The chatter within my mind was by turns screaming at me or unnervingly quiet.

The neurologist would later explain to me that the left side of one's brain controls the neurological pathways to the right side of one's body. The migraine on the right side of my head, while severe, was more like icing on the cake but not the true reason behind the numbing effect travelling down my body's right side. It was the lesions on the left side of my brain, due to MS, that caused brain damage as well as the paralysis down my right side, and it pulled me from life as I had known it. Yet in all that silence and then noise, in all that confusion and fear, I sensed the left side of my brain surrendering and letting go. At times, I also sensed a flicker of deep love, a feeling of being connected to the *universal source of All energy*. With determination in what seemed to be a repetitive scenario of two steps forwards and three steps backwards in my healing, I chugged along in first gear. Slowly, an inner perception awakened within me, a feeling of being *One* with the universe. In my own personal evolution, as I let go of my initial expectations for my life, I became able to walk through the suffering of this incurable, neurological autoimmune disease, and found the spiritual awareness of my authentic self. This was the power within my soul.

We each have this power within us, and it is my dream that sharing these words will nourish the Divine seeds planted long ago deep within all our spirits—our souls—and help us grow. Like the giant oak trees in my garden that are close to two hundred years old: They too, grew from a tiny seed, an acorn. I can hold that acorn in the palm of my hand; it does not look mighty or even strong, yet it is. The acorn already knows its own power, the power of the great oak within. No matter the storm winds that wildly blow, threatening the oak's existence, the oak stands rooted to the earth, facing the storm head on. Its branches bend with the winds, becoming one with the storm. It has life. We are each blessed with our own unique talents and strengths; they flow from the deepest parts of our souls and allow us to contribute lovingly to the world. They surface as we allow our souls to evolve.

The journey to find my destiny's new path was agonizing and confusing, but it was also exhilarating and exciting. One would think it would be a priority to reflect introspectively and nourish one's spirit, yet for many, including myself, before being diagnosed with MS, there seems to be this deadlock of unavailable time. We are too busy with too much to do, filling our moments with excessive *to-do lists*. It wasn't until I was forced through MS to absolute stillness of mind and body, that I realized my own foolishness in trying to control *my time*. I began to understand the power of stillness, silence, and reflection and the depth to be found in compassion, forgiveness, and love. These are the "food" sources that nourish our souls, reenergizing us as we heal from within.

My *new* destiny appeared as an unfathomable great mystery to me initially, but as I journeyed through my healing, I discovered all I needed was faith. The "universal flow" will guide me where I am meant to be as long as I follow my heart and soul. My own daily mission is to have courage with faith, patience with love, compassion with forgiveness, to remain open and part of the Divine flow that courses through us all.

It is my greatest dream that in sharing my journey it will help others seek and find inner peace from the challenges this disease presents.

Besides offering the reader a broader understanding of the emotional depths of this disease, I hope this story of someone who strives to live well—even with MS—brings inspiration.

Maureen Philpott Napier
Ontario, Canada

PART I

The Awakening Begins

Beloved

May your graces and light shine down upon me
Helping to illuminate the path to be
The focus of my life's worth
And how to better serve
Those surrounding me

I care so completely
So deeply
That at times, I lose my way
To give freely my love
In servitude to others
Is a natural response from the soul that is me
But how can it be, that I feel lost
Within the shadows of my love
As my energy plummets
It is the balance that I question, and seek
The stability within, that I desperately need
Then I can love fully and freely
Resonating this energy within our world
Like ripples upon the pond

The peace and happiness this would surely bring
Would be worth the life that is not my own
Loving and healing as I move on
For I am spirit and free to roam

Maureen Philpott Napier
March 15, 2006

CHAPTER I

The Chaos Before

March 26, 2006, seemed like any other normal day in our home. Rushed mornings, crammed with the task of getting my three young children dressed, fed, and readied for school, were always exhausting. Each day, something propelled us into a frantic state of chaos, no matter how organized and ready we thought we were the night before.

My youngest son, Alastair at six, would have preferred building his Lego creations, or Dinky Toy car-racing along my walls, than heading to school. Why I wondered could they not put on the clothing I'd neatly folded and placed at the bottom of their beds the night before? Why was it not good enough when Mum picked it, but *sick* (their new term for cool) when they picked it? Ainsley, eight at that time, was my drama queen and had an innate ability to create her own style of clothing and hair. I complained about her slow pace as she bunched her hair into miniature pigtails with differently coloured fuzzy elastics all over her head. I counted twelve pigtails! She spun in a circle, and the pigtails flew outward like a windmill. I was lost for words, which she always took as a good sign. Smiling, she dashed off to finish getting dressed. When she returned, I stood shocked—her creative ensemble actually looked amazing! Courtney, at eleven, seemed to be the only sane one, reminding us all that if we didn't hurry, *she'd* be late for school. Meanwhile, amidst the chaos, my husband, Terry, snored loudly in the distance. His shift work turned his days into nights and his nights into days, and I marveled that he managed to sleep at all. But the noise level never interfered with his ability to rest deeply and soundly.

I thought if I didn't have this blasted migraine on the right side of my head, which felt as if it were about to explode into a million pieces at any moment, I would be able to control the morning routine a little more smoothly. But all I could do was get through the moments, taking deep breaths, saying prayers, and begging for silence. The kids were ecstatic though, jumping, dancing, and twirling their "happy dance", as they put it. The cause for their celebration: Mum was driving them to school! (Normally, they were still dreaming when I headed for the door, around 5:30 AM most mornings.) Suddenly, our German shepherd, Koko, started barking, his tail wagging a violent drumbeat against the wall. *God help me!* I thought. *Now the dog has joined in!* I repeated my mantra to myself, *My migraine is getting smaller and smaller ... With each breath I take, I am getting stronger and stronger ...*

I sat down rather abruptly, holding my head like a ball, pulling my hair, and massaging my head at the same time. Little Alastair peeked in and looked at me under the fallen hair. We stared at each other upside down. He was matter-of-fact. "Don't puke on your shoes Mum; it will make me late for school". He was part way through grade one. Oh, to be six again!

Unfortunately, my children were used to my migraines and the effect they had on me. They were used to the dark glasses, the pain that could keep me collapsed in bed or sick in the bathroom, and even the need for absolute quiet and darkness when Mum had a migraine. They didn't blink an eye when I had one anymore; they had accepted them as part of normal life.

"Come on, Mum, time to go", they said. Ainsley and Alastair helped to heave me up from my chair, all three of them still doing their weird happy dances to the car. The bright sunshine made them even giddier. Spring had arrived!

I, on the other hand, was trying, unsuccessfully, to stop the bright sunshine from penetrating my eyeballs. I just needed some darkness, some silence, and if I could, to throw up—then, maybe I could get rid of this migraine. *No time,* I thought. I was already running behind schedule. I was always rushing, squeezing as much as I possibly could into my days and my nights, often complaining that I still didn't have enough time to do everything I needed to do.

So, as I drove my angels to school, my mind was filled with the chatter of meetings and deadlines, problem-solving plant-efficiency issues, creating new formulations and flavour profiles, laundry, what was I going to cook for dinner, business travel next week, and on and on—the list zoomed through my mind. My inner drive was broken down into an endless list of achieving, approving, and performing. The kids sang songs along with the radio and argued over who got to push the button to open the sunroof. As I dropped them off, I leaned my head against the steering wheel and prayed for strength to endure the migraine that was peaking to new levels of pain never before reached. A burning fire within my skull … but I had too much to do!

As a product development manager for a major food company, my days were always packed solid. More times than not, I lost weekends and early mornings due to product trials, equipment tests, business travel, or any combination thereof. My career as a research and development (R & D) food scientist spanned over twenty years, a field I thoroughly enjoyed. The creation of new products, the revision of others, the efficiency of plant production lines, and the sheer technical and physical demands of the work enthralled me. Life was good, although increasingly fast-paced, complex, and demanding. I was an organized and acutely driven individual who always sought success through external achievement. I thrived in the complexities within my life both professionally and personally, and what a ride it was! A roller coaster ride, called my life.

I had been battling that particular migraine for three days, but that also was not unusual for me. In fact, the day was going to be easier than most days, because I did not have to get to work before sun-up this morning. No plant trial deadlines loomed today. I could take the time to rest my head, hoping the migraine would eventually leave. I had no indication of the troubles that lay ahead.

Once at work and in my office, I remember staring at my Day-Timer, almost dazed. The organization of my time and duties were a well-oiled machine. Truth is, *I* was the machine, and I kept everything neatly moving forwards in an organized, controlled chaos. Running from one meeting to the next, helping operations, developing new formulations, purchasing or preparing new products for sensory evaluation, oh damn the mounds of paperwork … to name but a few in my endless lists. I scarcely had enough time to grab tea, never mind lunch! At the time, it didn't feel unmanageable; it was just the way things were. I was living in survival mode, unbeknownst to me, overwhelmed and in some way lost to life. I harboured a deeply ingrained belief in continuing one's obligation to reach pre-set goals and achieve externally-driven successes, no matter the cost to my health, or what else was going on in my life.

The constant doing and perfectionism within me not only drove my professional life, but also my personal life. I was the ship captain in my home, things ran smoothly when in my control and within my guidelines; everything had its place; everything perfectly cleaned, positioned and maintained … *my way.* I ran a tight ship. At work, I would have called these SOPs, standard operating procedures. I truly believed that these SOPs helped to keep things easy and running more smoothly within my family routines at home. I was always an in-tune organizer, anticipating and solving any and all problems that might surface. *I smiled to myself as I thought of the chaos that would ensue if they were left to their own devices.* The home would be a disaster in days, if not hours; it would be in complete disarray and anarchy. But I wondered, is perfectionism any better? Is doing *everything* for them any better? Who truly cared if the cushions on the couch were not placed diagonally at the corners? Or that the dust accumulated for a week instead of a couple of days, before being looked after? I realized now, a home is meant to be lived in, worn comfortably like your favourite old shoes, where warmth wraps around you and protects you so that you can unwind and rest. My home was always ready for a photo shoot in a glossy magazine spread, perfect, spotless, and managed … just like my life and projects at work.

As a driven overachiever, I had a deep need to do it all, and to try to do it all the right way the first time. My frantic pace culled any resemblance of inner peace. Professionally and personally, I was a great systematic multitasker and performer. Compounded by Terry's shift-work I felt the strain as if we were each single parents raising three young children like passing ships, as we rushed from one task to the next. The duties and needs that required my time, my energy seemed to balloon out of proportion to what I physically and mentally could do. But I had a hard time saying no to anyone, to do so felt like failure to me. I could not fail I could not let *them* down whomever *they* were. So I did the inevitable, I slept less, lived less, and did more, and then more. Running out of time I found myself speeding through my life faster than the speed of light. I needed more time! Doesn't that sound so familiar? Between professional and family (including the home) responsibilities I was running on empty, ranging anywhere from sixteen to eighteen hours on good days, or as the past couple of weeks had been much closer to twenty before I flopped into bed.

By lunchtime on that particular Tuesday, my migraine had consumed me. The pain was spreading within my head. But I had kept going, pushing through the pain and the throbbing that blurred my vision, as I usually did. When you have lived with migraines as long as I had—and I had them regularly, usually weekly—you have no choice but to develop a high pain threshold; you live your life working through them any way you can. My prescribed injections helped a little, but when the medication wore off, the migraine returned. It never occurred to me that what was happening to me might be more than that.

A typical migraine, my regular hell, the right side of my head was an exploding bomb, numbing the right side of my face. Pain radiated down the base of my head and neck, even nominal light had become extremely painful. My plan was to ride it out, knowing it would lift as the weather system changed, figuring the barometric pressure and temperature change was the cause of this one, as it consistently was.

At 1:45 PM, a tingling numbness started to travel down the right side of my body. I was in a product development meeting, trying to concentrate as the sensation crept down me. Tingling pins and needles. I asked a colleague sitting next to me, whom I knew to also suffer from migraines, if she had ever had tingling numbness that passed below her shoulders. She said no, so I thought I was imagining things. My mental confusion grew and I started second-guessing myself and the work I had just completed. The tingling got worse, but I pushed on, too caught up in my workload and getting the job done.

A few hours later, a quick email to a friend to ask what she thought got me a sudden and scary reply: "Not good, go to the hospital". *She's overreacting,* I thought. *I'm too busy!* I ignored her pleas to stop and get help. *It's just a migraine.* And I had suffered migraines for over twenty-three years. I kept going. I rushed here and there. I tried to ignore the feelings that crept down past my right hip. It was almost six before I rushed out of the office, racing home so my husband could leave for his job, just like normal.

I found it difficult to fold myself into my sporty, red, two-door car; it had never seemed so low to the ground before. On the way home, I had trouble getting my legs to operate the pedals in my standard-transmission. I eventually had to use my left leg to operate not only the clutch, but also the brake and gas pedals. Changing gears became a nightmare of panic and concentration before I succumbed to using my left hand to change gears. The confusion within my head was directly affecting my ability to drive my car safely. Once I got home, I thought of taking another injection, but something told me to call and ask the tele-health care system first. I was lucky to reach a nurse on the phone immediately.

I told her about the tingling and numbness on the right side of my body, the excruciatingly sharp pains circling within my head, but I didn't totally understand all the questions she asked me. My thoughts were confused, and I started to slur my words. Yes, I had pains in my back at the shoulder area. My heart started racing. Yes, my vision was blurring. Yes, I am dizzy and feel extremely weak. Within two minutes, that phone call swung my life in the opposite direction, and it would never be the same. My husband had been on his way out the door to work, thinking also it was just another migraine, when I told him, "They've sent an ambulance". He froze on the spot in total shock. I had to look away as his eyes silently questioned me.

The ambulance arrived, and I convinced the emergency crew that I didn't need a stretcher. Certainly I could walk to the ambulance—I had just driven home from work! Within a few short steps, though, I lost the use of my right leg. It was just gone. I couldn't make it move and I couldn't feel it. I couldn't tell if I even had a right leg. The paramedics caught me as I collapsed at the ambulance door.

Everything became blurred; I couldn't understand what people were asking me. I didn't know who—or what—I was. I couldn't remember my birth date when they asked. I was rushed to the hospital; en route, I heard that they thought I had suffered a stroke. I remember thinking,

But I just turned forty, how could I have had a stroke? Apparently, I remembered some things!

The night dragged on as they did multiple CAT scans that showed nothing. At least they ruled out stroke. The paralysis persisted, and the doctor thought it was due to the migraines. I relaxed—migraines always went away at some point.

I lay on a stretcher in the hallway of the emergency room, hooked up to an IV. I needed to let the migraine run its course. I was to be kept overnight for observation, so Terry returned home to explain and look after our children. As he left me, I buried my head under pillows *and* my coat, but the light and noise of the hospital kept penetrating my cocoon, and my agony only increased. I had another sleepless night, the third in a row.

Very early the next morning, I reluctantly called into work. "I'll be in late", I told them. I actually believed the words as they left my mouth. "I am in the hospital but hope to be out as soon as I get rid of the IV". They were more than understanding, and I could imagine my colleagues' shocked faces as they rolled into work one by one. They were part of my extended family, after all. You can't spend the amount of hours I did at work and not feel the deeper connection during projects and of unity with colleagues. Teamwork was always at the forefront of my leadership; a unified goal within the company for success. My own innate drive and passion to succeed was by far as addicting as any strong intoxicating drug.

The truth was, beneath my mental confusion and pounding pain, I had a sense of impending doom and wanted nothing more than to escape. I was in fight-or-flight panic mode, trying to evade the anxiety that my life was slipping away. If my legs had been capable of holding my body up, I would have left the hospital. I was battling the fear that something was terribly wrong, a deep fear that intensified as time passed by. But I couldn't accept what was happening to me, so I was fighting for my very life. All I could think to do was what came naturally: to use my own unceasing compulsion to accomplish something, to push against the boundaries of what I bear. The sudden fear building within me knocked me breathless; my knowledge and experience meant nothing.

"I can't stay in the hospital", I told the doctor. "It just won't fit into my schedule". He just raised his eyebrows, as if amused by my remark.

Hours passed in the hallway. Slowly. And as they passed, so did my strength. Weakness pulled me into a vortex of spasm and pain. All I could do was curl up and hold my head, praying that it would soon stop. Fear turned to heartache and despair. I understood how pain could get you to a point of suicide. I had no relief, no help to guide me. No soft touch to let me know I was okay. The doctor and nurses seemed distant and cold. Each time they came to check my vitals, I recoiled. They repeatedly flashed lights into my eyes, making my head explode like fireworks. No soft words to give me strength. Their harsh tones held no compassion; they showed no understanding that their raised voices crippled me, that their questions confused me. No quiet, no privacy. The drugs they fed me intravenously did nothing. In too much pain to think, desolation and worry swirled beyond my control, beyond rationality. It occurred to me that this may be the end of my life, and I only survived one breath at a time.

Finally, Terry appeared in the ER, after having dropped our children off at school. I literally grabbed him. I begged him to take me home, to save me. The hospital situation was making things worse! I pleaded with the ER doctor to let me go home, and since they thought it was all migraine-related, he agreed. I called into work and finally admitted I wouldn't get in that day. "But hopefully tomorrow, if the migraine leaves!" The gentle voice at the other end of the phone simply encouraged me to rest and not to worry about anything. Easier said than done. But my body was calling the shots now, not my mind.

Late morning, March 27, Terry took me home and put me to bed—finally, the complete darkness and quiet that I needed. I had no knowledge of the time that passed. My very reality—except for extreme pain—was lost to me. I must have slept.

By the next day, most of the migraine on the right side of my head had gone—though the paralysis had not. I couldn't walk without dragging my right leg. It felt severed from the rest of my body. My whole right side felt separate from me. Even my head, which was no longer engulfed in migraine, throbbed with an on-again-off-again burning sensation on the left side of my head that I can only describe as electric. It was like a light switch flicking on and off.

Believe it or not, I worked from home the evening of the twenty-eighth, trying to get caught up in all the tasks that I had fallen behind on the previous two days. It was frustrating because I was finding it hard to concentrate—like I was in a dense fog. I could not recall simple mathematics, ingredients, or scientific formulations that I had used for over twenty years. I fought hard to remember the number "2"! I had a sense of what it was, but I could not put a visual to it—what did it look like? I remember the shock of admitting that to myself, but I pushed it away. I continued to attribute all my symptoms to the after-effects of the migraine.

I could barely see through my right eye, as if I were looking through frosted glass. Flashing spots of grey and white would come and go. I banged into walls and doors dragging my body around and reaching for handles that were either farther or closer than they looked. Well after midnight, I finally gave up and fell into bed, then tossed and turned the rest of the night in agony.

I had told work I'd be in after my family doctor's visit on the morning of the twenty-ninth. But by then, I had a complete split down the middle of my body—drawn like a fine line from the tip of my head to the tip of my toes. I could neither move nor feel my right side, the pins and needles replaced with *nothingness*. I could not even drag myself around anymore. I used Terry as my crutch to get from our bedroom to the bathroom and then to the kitchen. That was when I lost all rational thought. I continued to think it would get better by itself …any time now. Not able to accept the reality of my paralysis, I ignored the signs my body and brain produced and pushed myself to carry on as always. *No pain, no gain—just do it!* If there were roadblocks, I would climb them. I couldn't drive myself to my doctor's appointment, since my car was a standard and my right leg was useless, not to mention trying to change gears with a nonresponsive right arm! So I searched in the drawer for the keys to my husband's automatic Honda Odyssey. One leg operating two pedals was a lot easier than trying to make my left leg work three pedals.

Terry stood like a statue, arms crossed over his chest in front of our side door, blocking my way to the minivan. He ranted and raved at how stubborn I was, how idiotic I was to think I could drive myself to the doctor. "You are completely insane!" he yelled.

I remember thinking that I could not have this battle with him on top of everything else. *Just get out of my way; I am fine!* I thought to myself. I had a fierce independence and rarely if ever asked for help. Losing my independence was one of the first hurdles I would have to overcome. I counterattacked with my usual line, "It's called 'being positive' and 'having determination!'" But they came out of my mouth in a slurred whisper.

"I have a few more words for it", he assured me. His hair was standing straight up like a porcupine, his face darkened with stubble and his eyes from exhaustion and worry. He couldn't even get his shirt tucked in all the way. But he was adamant, his strength dredged from the core of him. His mind might be racing, he told me, but mine wasn't working at all.

He was right. My mind was a jumble. I didn't understand much about what was happening, but I knew I needed his help, his strength, and his compassion. I surrendered and let him drive me to the doctor.

Once there, I endured more bloodwork and echocardiograms of my heart. I still had no diagnosis. My family doctor told Terry he had arranged for a neurologist to see me at the hospital. So, back we went, and I was admitted again. *There goes my weekend!* I thought. I called my office and relayed what little knowledge I had, still hopeful I would be back to "normal" by Monday. I don't remember all that I said. I don't remember their response. Things had become a blur. I was having difficulty understanding *what* people were saying to me, never mind remembering it. And I had extreme difficulty speaking. Everyone seemed to be talking so fast. I couldn't keep up.

But the guilt! It hit me like a cement block. I felt I had failed everyone around me: my colleagues, my children, my husband, and even myself. How could I look after my children and maintain our family routines? How could I handle the workload at the office? There was too much work, too many projects now left in limbo, because I couldn't get my body or my brain to work. Then I remembered I was supposed to go to Vancouver on business the following week.

My brain overloaded. Intense pain surged through my head like a tidal wave of my failures, consuming me. I grasped my skull, trying to contain the explosions that were ripping me apart. Besides the disease that was taking over my life, a disease I barely knew existed, I was embroiled in a psychological battle of fear, despair, and guilt. A battle I could ill afford. It wasted energy I didn't have. I was sinking in a toxic soup that poisoned my spirit and my soul—and I was the bloody chef!

One Soul to Another

Silence, at times, is all I have
As I await direction and strength
The stillness within provides to me
Divine power and love
I find I have the ability
To quietly build myself up once again
The noise surrounds me
Making the silence even more important
As I struggle to think clearly
Deeply search within my feelings
To understand what this lesson
Reveals to me
I realize I am not alone
For you have come, as you have done before
To sit quietly with me
An Angel, with a familiar face
She fills me with renewed energy
One soul to another
One love to another
Confusion fits in between the spaces
Emotional holes I have found
I sense not my thoughts
As I struggle to let out
What is hidden beneath my surface

But it is enough to know that you are there
Enough to know that you really care
The smile on your face tells me not to worry
Your warm embrace
Reminds me to have faith
And when I am not sure what to say
I know you understand anyway
One soul to another
One friend to another
One love to another
It is enough to have you with me
The rest will wait
The silence will break
One more hour, one more day
With you by my side, I know I'm okay.

Maureen Philpott Napier
April 2006

CHAPTER 2

The Testing

March 30, 2006. I had been lying on a stretcher in the emergency ward's special "waiting room" for over twenty-four hours. A good dozen patients, including myself, waited for a bed in the overcrowded hospital. Nurses were few and far between, administering medication, checking vitals, and disappearing into the too-bright hollows again. I had held out as long as I could before asking for help—I pushed the call button and waited. Nothing happened. No one came. There I was, hooked up to an IV, heavily medicated, one side of me dragged around by the other, my vision coming and going, and unable to wait any longer. Mother Nature was finished calling; I had to use the bathroom. I pulled my body off the stretcher and used my IV pole like a cane to stabilize my unsteady, one-sided shuffle. Luckily, I was the closest of the bunch of us to the washroom and made it just as a nurse was entering the room. The few steps I'd managed completely exhausted me, but we simply exchanged smiles, and I closed the door behind me.

Everything went well enough until I had to get to the sink to wash my hands. I had to let go of the IV pole—a big mistake. I was much too unsteady for that. A sharp pain like a knife to my head sent me to the floor. Somehow, while I was collapsing, I managed to grab the emergency cord. Then I was out.

When I came to, I was still on the floor of the washroom. No one had come. The emergency button flashed on and off; all I could do now was bang on the door. Apparently, there had been a shift change—no one was monitoring the station where the emergency flasher continued to beep. It was only thanks to Jim, a patient I had befriended next to me, who alerted the nurse to my banging, that I finally got the help I needed. By the time she found me, I was far beyond my body's exhaustion.

Two more days crawled by in the waiting room, and each day brought a barrage of tests. They did little but confuse and drain me. Terry would come in to check on me and bring me up to speed on our children and how they were all coping, but I couldn't remember which tests I had undergone already and which were still to come. He kept the children's regular routine as it always had been—minimizing other changes helped them cope with having Mum in the hospital. But the weight fell heavily on Terry's shoulders. What with school, horseback riding, tutors, martial arts, and then evening visits with me, it was quite a balancing act! Our children had not seemed initially fazed by my hospitalization. They brought cards and pictures they made especially for me. The girls told me about the horses and their lessons. Alastair told me how much the horses pooped and how much it had "stank"! Some things hadn't changed at all.

Each time they left, I was swallowed by a deep sorrow. I couldn't connect well with people because of the ongoing language difficulties. I couldn't understand them; they couldn't understand me. The paperwork I was asked to sign made no sense to me either, but I was told as a patient admitted to the hospital I had to sign it. Though I never really knew what it all meant, I managed to scribble a signature as directed. So much for "informed consent". I felt so alone. The despair would hit me and I hadn't the strength to fight it. The onslaught of tests continued. They drained so much blood from me for testing I was damn sure I had none left. I faded into the distance as if I weren't even there.

My own brain tortured me, relentlessly replaying the thought that I was failing everyone around me. A confused and continuous loop, my failure consumed me. I was worried about everything and anything. Timetables and reports of projects, appointments, and plant trials; schedules of the kids' routines at school, at home, and their extracurricular activities flooded my mind all at once and at lightning speed. The driven perfectionist within me was screaming to get going, *just do it*. But my body continuously responded, *NO!* The more I struggled, the more pain and the deeper my despair. I became so anxious I couldn't breathe, my heart raced; I felt like I was choking. The duty nurse with a compassionate voice tried to lead me through it with deep breaths, but I kept screaming in my head, *Help me!* No words came out my mouth as my inability to communicate jettisoned any rationality within my thinking process. They eventually put me on a drug to calm me as well as the sporadic anxiety attacks that hit me.

I started writing to escape the feeling of frustration that surged through me. In the past few years, I had used this technique many times, and somehow it reminded me that in order to release my fear I needed to have faith and let go. I repeated to myself, *Breathe. Let go. Everything will be fine.* I soon realized I was not worried about myself so much as my colleagues, my friends, and of course my family. I felt ashamed and helpless; I knew that this was bringing an unexpected burden to their already busy lives. At first, the hopelessness of my situation increased my despair at not being able to be there for my colleagues and family. Ultimately, though, I understood there was nothing I could do—physically or mentally—for anyone else. This was a huge realization: *I did not need to do it all.* Once I truly accepted that, I was better able to breathe through my frustrations and anxiety attacks. A giant step in letting go! They would have to manage any way they could. Now I could start trying to heal *me*. That powerful understanding caused a huge shift in how I perceived my need to help others and "do it all".

As the days passed, I tried to think positive thoughts. I would look around me and see others in their own distress, and I would send them my silent prayers for a speedy recovery. I would thank all those who came my way to help me, even if it was just washing the floors or emptying the garbage. I was filled with gratitude for those who bathed me, opened the food packages on my tray as they served me lunch, everyone who helped me when I could not physically help myself. I used visualization techniques to aid in my healing and imagined myself walking in a field of long grass with the sun shining brightly and the ocean waves crashing ashore in the distance as my children ran and played alongside me. As I carried on, moment-by-moment creating something positive in my situation, new moments of inner balance would *start* to surface.

My sense of humour became a saving grace. I had days when I laughed at all the crazy things I was worried about before. I pictured myself as a starfish stuck on the beach, out of my element and unable to move one whole side. I was still stranded on a stretcher in the waiting room—four days later and a bed was still not available. I had flashes of wearing my white lab coat backwards, more like a straitjacket than a uniform! I had two choices: laugh or cry. For now, I chose to laugh—there would be many days ahead for more tears to fall.

The tests continued. The neurologist had more gizmos in his *knapsack* than I had kitchen utensils. I remembered thinking, *Where is his doctor's bag? Since when do they use knapsacks?* He lifted up my right leg as I looked on, and the sensation of not feeling that leg really hit me. *Is that my leg?* I wanted to yell at him, "Excuse me, I am not a steak; I do not need tenderizing!" But I didn't; I stayed quiet as he poked and prodded me, something I'd been enduring for days. It was still so hard to talk normally that I had withdrawn into myself. The language confusion on the receiving end would come and go, but rarely could I get my thoughts to properly come *out* of my mouth, an embarrassment that fueled my silence.

The neurologist looked up to the ceiling so many times I was sure part of my right side must be stuck up there too. But, thank God, my left eye still worked—all that was up there were cobwebs. I never heard what he said. I was too busy wondering why the sprinkler head in the ceiling of a hospital room would be encased in old cobwebs. My mind had resumed its rambling. I thought, *The firemen would not be happy about those cobwebs!* Then I heard him say something and reality brought me back: I needed more tests. More CAT scans, more bloodwork, more echocardiograms, ultrasounds, and an MRI (magnetic resonance imaging). I waited for results for so many tests that I finally gave up counting the number and the wait time. The information made no sense to me. They could have been speaking a different language for all I knew.

At last, Terry was at my side during one of the neurology exams, which meant information was being passed to someone who could not only remember it, but also process it. I read the frustration on his face. He wanted answers too. It had been a week of not knowing, and the uncertainty and helplessness scared him. The children were asking questions for which we had no answers. It had become hard to look at the specialists, knowing they did not have any answers for us either.

I had taken to calling all of these specialists "Doctor", as if they were a single entity. I could never remember their names and, after awhile, it didn't seem any more important than what time it was. But knowing they were confused too, added to our fear and hopelessness. Once again, I looked around me and picked someone I thought needed "extra help"—like the woman who had suffered a stroke and her attendant family drowning in a constant wail of tears. I prayed to give them strength and love and found that it helped me become aware of my capacity to be strong through these difficulties I faced.

April 4, a bed had finally become available, so I was to be moved to a room. The doctor appeared and told us the MRI had showed inflamed darker regions on my brain, as well as inflammation on my upper and lower spine. He put me on a heavy dose of steroids to help decrease the inflammation in all areas as quickly as possible. Then he said he wanted to do another MRI—this one with dye—and retest my whole spine and brain. This test would produce more results from the areas on my brain that concerned him and help him understand what was going on. I didn't understand, but by now I was too exhausted to care. Life had slowed to a crawl, and I was living in a dense fog of extreme pain. I didn't know who *I* was anymore. And I truly did not care.

I got through the days by scribbling down my thoughts as poems—or even just one sentence or two—to feed my faith and give me hope that I would be whole again. And I mean scribbling. I was right-handed, unfortunately, and my dominant side was numb! So, writing with my left hand turned out almost illegible scribbling. I would have to make sense of what these jumbles of words meant later.

Pain surged through my body, but I couldn't tell where it came from. Originally, morphine was used in my IV to reduce the pain, but I reacted poorly to it, losing my sense of self even more. It gave me nightmares and night/day terrors that only increased my sense of doom. I eventually refused it and opted for other ways to help me get through the pain. These burning electrical impulses were testing my resolve. When it got too intense, I was given injections to ease the pain and help me sleep. The nurse asked me which cheek I wanted the next round of needles to go into. I looked at her and laughed, "That's easy, my right side—I feel nothing there anyway". We both laughed and, for a few moments, I felt like my old self again. Until she had to roll me over, because of course I couldn't do that either!

The phantom pains increased and, for the remainder of my hospital stay, I would get injections every four to six hours to ease their sharpness, but in reality the medication did little. The pain continued to peak. I remembered the breathing techniques I'd used while I was in labor with Courtney, my first child. Doing them helped somewhat, but I think mainly because it helped to stabilize my erratic heartbeat.

Panic and confusion would take control over me from time to time. But I reminded myself to enjoy the view from my bedside window. I was lucky; it was of the lake, and I could visually distract myself as the days rolled on.

I had a lot of time to myself between the visitors, nurses, and doctors. Initially, that scared me. I had not been a person who had designated any time for being *stationary* and *alone* with her own thoughts and feelings. How could I? I had three small children and a demanding career. One moment, I was a strong, independent, career-driven mother always surrounded by nuclear family, friends, or coworkers. The next, I was alone on a bed where I did not even have the ability to look after myself. I was used to helping others, but not in being helped. That radical shift scared the hell out of me.

April 6, 2006. I was still in the unknown as to what had happened to me. But when I was alone, I was more aware of the troubles within my head. I did not completely understand it, but I knew there were issues that were getting worse. The head pain was prolonged by noise levels and light. My language skills, including speech and thought, were somehow affected: I was aware that sometimes my speech was slurred. Plus, I couldn't grasp what the nurses were saying to me. Worst of all, when I talked, I lost what it was I was trying to say; the words just didn't come easily. I remember feeling completely stupid as I tried to search for the words I needed within my mind.

Both thinking and talking had become a laborious chore. I had to really concentrate to get the words to go from my thoughts to my mouth, and sometimes even that failed me. Auditory understanding remained sporadic. Some moments, I understood, just a little slower than usual. Other moments, I did not have a clue, truly lost within my own mind.

External noise and light—from the hallways or the lights in my room—continued to blindside me with extreme head pain. Its strength dominated me beyond any of my worst migraine pain, but was now located only on the left side of my head. These issues magnified my fear, for I could not control them. Once again, I sensed I had lost all control of my life.

Terry visited me daily and went with me to radiology for the MRI-with-dye procedure. As one technician was placing me onto the machine bed, I could see Terry talking to the other technician through the glass window. He waved, but all I could do was smile, because they had strapped me down to prevent any movement. The pain at this time was tolerable and I could breathe through the peaks. The technician gave me a panic button to hold in case I needed the machine to stop for any reason. It sounded straightforward enough, and the process began. Within seconds, my head erupted. The clanging from the machine and the lights in the chamber magnified the pain beyond imagination. It felt as if a bomb had gone off inside my skull. I couldn't catch my breath. I desperately wanted to hold my head and curl up into a ball, but the restraints stopped my ability to do so. I don't remember pushing the panic button, but I do remember the chamber bed sliding out from the vast machine. Tears streamed down my face as I gasped for air. It took me a few minutes to become fully aware of my surroundings again. The throbbing consumed everything within me.

Without knowing, I had pressed the panic button and never released it. I had been in the chamber for less than twenty seconds. It felt like an eternity. Once I was calmed, the technicians placed towels over my face so the lights would not aggravate my head pain. But there was nothing they could do for the noise of the machine. If you've never had an MRI, it sounds like a train with something stuck in the tracks. I was already wearing earplugs, but that did not reduce the noise enough. There was no other way around the testing. I needed that MRI to help find what was wrong with me. Armed with that knowledge, I managed to agree to go back into the machine; more prepared the second time for the inevitable clash. I told the technician not to give me the panic button. I did not trust myself not to use it when my pain spiked. There was a fireball in my skull that ignited all my nerve endings, electrifying the pain as it shot down the right side of my body, from my neck to my toes. The pain was beyond anything I had ever endured, even with severe migraines.

When it was over, I was semiconscious, largely unaware of what was happening to me. But I do remember Terry coming to my side and telling me, "It's over now. You're okay". I focused on him—his familiarity, his concern. And I felt the strain leaving my body.

He told me he had seen my "brain develop" on the monitor. "It had dots and was shining bright as a Christmas tree!" He seemed to think that was very cool.

I knew I was coming back around when I thought, *This guy is nuts!*

As we headed back to my hospital room, Terry brought me up to speed on household events. He knew I was weakened from that testing and did most of the talking, allowing me to rest and recover. With the help of friends, the children were looked after at night. Then Terry would head off to his nightshift at work. He never once complained to me about the extra burden that this caused him, never once complained of his own exhaustion, or the fact that it looked like he was going to have a disabled wife who needed fulltime care. He was always cheerful; his devotion and compassion gave me strength when I felt so weak. He believed in me and didn't give up on me, even when I momentarily gave up on myself. I relaxed about the care of our children—it seemed like they were handling the situation much better that I was.

It had now been eleven days since my initial admission, and there was still no diagnosis. I often felt so very much alone, even with all the noise and activity fluttering around me from the hospital. But then something happened, and an inner feeling of stillness and silence *started* to feed my soul. I lay back on my hospital bed, closed my eyes, and slowly reflected on what life was for me now. With deep breathing, I would again create a calm space, and then pull into my imagination a vision of my whole, healthy body. I would then envision myself doing Tai Chi. That visualization started to help me navigate through the maze of my own thoughts. It became a way of taking charge of my healing, and I gained strength to get through the endless days.

> "Never give up on yourself or feel shame as a result of not fulfilling your objective to serve as a being of inspiration. Every fall that you take is a gift, and every relapse is a glorious opportunity."
>
> ~Dr. Wayne Dyer~

From time-to-time, fear would raise its ugly head, and I would be forced to stare into the eyes of the unknown. Despair's darkened hell would engulf me—mind, body, and soul—where I fought for each breath I took. It felt as though I had fallen into a giant darkened pit, where there seemed to be no way out. All this was compounded by the doctors' inability to diagnose what was wrong with me. The fear of these unknowns was a powerful enemy.

Yet, as I continued with my visualizations, I found I did have the ability to face fear and to reframe it as only a passing feeling. As my old identity was ripped from my core, a hunger grew within me, flickers of life within death. With that surrendering and that acceptance, the fear very slowly began to drain away. I frequently repeated in silence, *This too, in time, shall pass,* until I could breathe more easily and stare into that bottomless hell of fear, knowing all was as it should be. It was this deepening faith that guided me through my darkest of moments like the North Star in the middle of the night or a lighthouse near rocky and stormy seashores. It brought me some comfort and peace even when there was only a flicker of light. My self-determination to stay positive and to succeed also helped steer me in the right direction. I was not a quitter, no matter how rough the stormy seas. I knew I would find a way. I knew I was a survivor.

Watch and Learn

The winds pick up
See the trees below
I watch and surrender
As the performance grows

Waves rush ashore
A storm brews and says hello
Birds vanish
As they sense the increasing difficulty
In flying with winds against their tails

How is it they survive?
When storms hit unrepentantly
How can they live on?
And fear not the next storm

What can I learn from them?
That will help me get along
With the storms in my life
As they consume and swallow me whole
I close my eyes, and feel the storm
Becoming *One* with the unknown

Maureen Philpott Napier
April 2006

CHAPTER 3

The Discovery

On April 7, 2006, the morning began with a glorious sunrise. I watched the colours creep above the lake. Injection time and the noise from the hallway awakened me from what little sleep I had had. But that day, I didn't mind. My heart and soul drank in the beauty of the sunrise. I felt great … until I realized I should use the washroom. An exhausting expedition—it could be Mount Everest, it felt so daunting.

Since I had fallen three times, I was supposed to call the nurse. It seemed even that dignity had been taken from me. But I was a determined fool. I calculated how I could get from my bed to the wheelchair. Just like coming up with product trials, I ran through my head different ways I might flop into the blasted thing. I tried to get up, but as my left arm pulled to get the rest of me off the bed to a sitting position, I realized I was already exhausted. And I still hadn't gone to pee! My body was totally drained, as if I had just finished a long-distance marathon. It practically screamed in agony, yet I had barely moved. I finally gave in, fell back onto the bed, and pressed the call button for the nurse.

Since I had no feeling whether or when Mother Nature was now calling, I had been using the clock to gauge myself. Then I would sit and wait, praying that sooner or later my body, which had stopped working and feeling, could somehow remember the sensation of sitting on the toilet, and then let me go! It's stupid really, but I refused the bedpan for many reasons. Foremost among them being that I couldn't feel a damn thing on my right side, so how could I lift my ass in the air for a bedpan?

As I waited for the nurse to arrive, I thought of the fact that a month ago I had turned forty and was personally and professionally at the top of my game. Turning forty never fazed me; it was just a number. But many around me at work had joked, "It's all downhill from here, Moe". I had laughed alongside them at the time, hoping for a slow walk downhill, not a race at two hundred kilometers an hour. I mean, who was I in a race with anyway? I made a mental note to pay them back—they must have jinxed me! Then it hit me that I did need that white coat with the buttons and arms in the back—who else has a rambling conversation with themselves when they are on the toilet?

Later that day, Terry strolled in with our Tim Hortons coffees, and I proceeded to get caught up in all the family news. One hour later, the neurologist walked in. I assumed he had the results of all those bloody tests, and I hoped he wouldn't look as puzzled as he did his last visit. I grabbed Terry's hand as we stared at the doctor's face looking for good news. My heart was racing and my hand sweating. The neurologist was young, probably in his early thirties; he wore a crisp white lab coat similar to my own and had a tan I envied. I looked into his deep brown eyes and waited. It seemed like an eternity passed, and then my fate was determined.

His diagnosis was dispassionate. I felt the shivers run up my left arm into my neck as he coldly stated, "You have multiple sclerosis, also termed MS, a progressively destructive form, a neurological disease, which has no cure".

He told us I had multiple lesions on the left hemisphere of my brain, causing brain damage. He explained again the role of the left lobe, which affects the right side of the body, my thinking processes, my memory, and my speech. What Terry had originally thought was "cool"—the way my brain "lit up like a Christmas tree" on the MRI with dye—was actually the lesions, caused by MS, which left me with significant brain damage to the left hemisphere of my brain. With multiple sclerosis my immune system makes antibodies to proteins which damage the myelin sheath covering the nerve endings. This inflammation then disrupts the transmission of electrical impulses, thus causing permanent or partial loss of sensation or muscle function. Damage along my spinal cord, crossing over both the left and right sides, was due to progressive tissue (myelin sheath) impairment, and dysfunction of these electrical impulses to complete tasks my brain was trying to send. He believed, from the amount of damage I had, that I had lived with this disease for well *over* a decade!

Terry and I listened in shocked silence as he relayed his prognosis. Since damage to both sides of my spine had already taken place, I could lose the ability to use both my legs; in short I could end up needing a motorized wheelchair as I lost my ability to control the motor skills of my limbs. Brain damage would continue my onslaught of difficulties with memory, communication and thinking processes. At that point, time stopped. I don't remember what else he said. One moment he was there, the next he was gone. And as he walked out of my hospital room, so did the life I had previously lived.

My husband asked at the nurses' station if they had any more in-depth information on MS. We knew so little, and what the neurologist had relayed to us was already a ball of confusion to both of us. The nurse on duty was kind enough to print off material from the MS Society's website, so my husband and I could figure out what the diagnosis truly meant. But it was not the time to absorb more details on the disease; we were both still in shock. We had heard of the disease, but only on the most superficial level. We were both still lost. As Terry related some of the information we had been given, my mind—already having difficulty working—shut down. It still seemed as though everyone was speed-talking in a foreign language. I withdrew into myself—the inner war seemed complete.

How could I fight a disease of this magnitude? The damage was already done; it would now only get progressively worse. MS affected my brain's operations, my spinal column's operations, and my immune system, to name but a few consequences. This neurological disease would progressively attack my body, and it had no cure. I not only felt completely lost, I *had* lost. It was as if the disease waved its victory flag in front of me and demanded my unconditional surrender.

My own confusion escalated, and the quietness of the room was unnerving. I remember saying to my husband, "Oh, I'm fine, don't worry", but deep down inside, the panic and fear took grip. I kept thinking, *Don't cry, not yet; wait till he's gone.* Initially, I tried to protect Terry, my children, my friends, and even myself from the true extent of what was raging inside me. My love for them fueled my protectiveness. I did not want them to hurt alongside me. But by the same token, I also did not truly understand what I was feeling, except for deep confusion, fear, and then emptiness. To try to grasp the ramifications, my mind constantly replayed the doctor's diagnosis. "You have MS … There is no cure". Until at one point, there was nothing left to replay. No thoughts that I was aware of. No feelings of happiness or sorrow. No awareness of any emotion at all. Just emptiness. In retrospect, I think that slowed my recovery. Delaying the emotions that raged through my soul only made me feel more alone.

Terry couldn't stay long. His outside commitments with our children, their activities, our home, and his job now all dropped on his shoulders. Talk about sink or swim. I knew the hardship he was dealing with. I wondered how much longer he could go on with that stress, on top of everything else. Right now, he had to go pick up the kids from school. He kissed me and told me everything would be fine. I nodded and smiled, making sure not to burden him with my raging fears. But as he left, I stared out my window. Such a normal day, the sun shining down. The lake was a brilliant blue, and seagulls flew over the beach. I could see people walking hand in hand, enjoying the wonder of spring as my life crashed down around me. As the remaining hours crept by, I did little but stare outside, the emptiness consuming me. I instinctively knew I was bottling it up inside, yet I hadn't a clue how to open up and let the pain out. At the time, I didn't even care. I withdrew from life, for life had withdrawn from me. Once again, I had unconsciously put myself at the bottom of the list.

That time in my life was one of the darkest moments I had ever faced. We didn't tell friends or family until the next day, partly because we were still in shock. We both needed time to absorb the information. The hours that followed were a combination of deep despair, loss, fear, and enormous guilt. With that diagnosis, it was as if the very breath I needed to survive had been sucked out of me. It was indeed difficult to see or feel even a flicker of light within me. I now knew I was never going to be who I had been before, that person had just died. From the information the nurses gave us, I knew the basics of this autoimmune disease: with progressive multiple sclerosis, the disease would only continue to damage my brain functions, my motor skills, and my immune system. I was not prepared for the permanent loss of the person I had been for forty years or for the impact that the disease would have on all our lives or for the aftershocks that would rattle my very soul.

"Within my darkest despair, and deepest suffering, lay the tools and lessons that would unlock the essence of my true self.
This would become the greatest
awakening of my soul".

~ Maureen Philpott Napier ~
2006

Chapter 4

The Release

One of my regular nurses was supposed to come on duty later that afternoon, and I so wanted to see her. I was drawn to her somehow. Before my diagnosis, I had laughed and joked with her and many other nurses that cared for me. It was my way of releasing the uncertainty and fear. They told me I was the *life* of the ward. It seemed I made them enjoy their shift a little more, and they helped me remember my old self a little more. Both of us won. Some days, these interactions were all that kept me thinking positively. We laughed when I managed to get my wheelchair stuck in a corner, and when I felt nauseous for repeatedly going in circles. Finally, they explained to me that I was only using my left arm and left leg to propel myself forwards. My brain couldn't even grasp the logistics. Yet here I was, driving in circles, going fast, and going nowhere. I made a sign and put it on my wheelchair: CAUTION: NEW DRIVER. And promptly told a couple of the therapists that they should supply training manuals for these new-fangled wheels! Those were the days prior to diagnosis, when I promised myself to *think positively* and give back to the staff who worked so tirelessly on the ward I was on. It was the surgical ward, and too many patients took advantage of the call buttons way too often. I tried to lighten my spirits as well as those around me, and it had worked well … until now.

Darkness had fallen by the time nurse Peggy walked into my room and stood by my bed, that emptiness still looming within me. We looked at each other for a few moments before she sat on my bed and explained why it had taken her so long to come and see me. She'd had difficulty facing me. She said her heart sank when she had read my chart at the start of her shift, "Diagnosis—MS". I don't know why, but her words gave me the key I needed to unlock my feelings. The tears flowed out of me and wouldn't stop. She held me in her arms, and we cried together. She offered me compassion, love, and hope. She was the first person to witness my humble falling. I felt naked, broken down, as if my heart had been literally ripped from me. In that moment of complete surrender, the driven perfectionist, the overachiever who was always in constant motion and self-control, died along with those grieving tears. Throughout the night, she brought heated blankets to ease the shivering I could not control, made me tea, and helped me hold the cup to my lips. Peggy nursed me with compassion and understanding. Maybe because she was mostly a stranger, it was easier to crumble. I did not have to pretend all was well, and I didn't feel the guilt of burdening a loved one.

I let the tears fall like a thundering waterfall and grieved a life that was now gone. All I could think about was my inability to walk unaided and all the personal care I could no longer do on my own. I knew I would never be the independent career woman or active mum I once had been. My God, I was stuck on a bed unless someone helped me up! My body was crippled, my brain was slower, and I'd lost many of my fine motors skills due to the neurological damage. The realization that this disease was not going to get better, but would actually worsen seemed to me a death sentence for whom I had been. My life, my work, my very own identity was now forever changed. I could not rationalize these thoughts, the physical pain merged with the mental anguish of my previous life that was now lost forever.

Over the next few days, all I did was cry. The tears would not stop, the ache in my heart continued, and I found myself releasing all that had accumulated inside me. The despair that had been filling me finally burst its banks and flooded everything. I let it flow freely and privately, some part of me knowing that in time I would pick up the pieces and move on to the next stage. But for now, I understood I needed to grieve, cleanse, and weep not only because of a disease but also because of a life I had lived for forty years. And it was indeed a healing power that washed over me. As I cried, it rained heavily outside as well, and I thanked God for crying with me. That's how it felt at the time. The waves on the lake crashed ashore, and I watched them, feeling that the storm and I shared something in common: an inner turmoil powerful enough to create white caps on the lake, as the tears from heaven fell all around. I was thankful for the rain and waves, for I would close my red, swollen eyes and pretend that all my fear and pain were being washed away, and that I would soon be able to face the path that lay before me.

The darkness within me and around me seemed to swallow me whole at times. Some moments, it was all I could do to get past that despair one breath at a time. I seemed to slip into oblivion where the chronic pain and mental confusion only followed me. There was no escape. I looked everywhere within me for one, hoping and praying that next time I opened my eyes, I could laugh: all a bad dream.

It had now been fifteen days since my initial admission to the hospital, but it felt like years. I have never in all my life been so physically and mentally exhausted, as if the very energy I needed to survive had drained from me. It would hit me in waves. I was never prepared for the intensity and at times I wished I had been called to God's home instead. I did not want to live with this pain, this crumbled, paralyzed body, this foggy brain. I was angry I had to live my life that way. I was angry I couldn't figure it out and fix it. I was angry at ... me! My body had failed me, my mind had failed me, and now I questioned my soul. Would that fail me too?

Those first three days after my diagnosis were the hardest to cope with. I battled a dark and cold despair at hell's door and felt so alone I knew I battled for my very life. To others, though, I appeared reserved, quiet, and as in control as always. I even kept my battles to myself.

I turned to writing as I had done before. Though I had never thought of myself as *a writer*, it seemed that my creative side, which I had somewhat been unaware of, would seek its own passage. I had written some poetry prior to this sudden life shift, but not at the scale hitting me now. What would flow from me seemed to have a purpose of its own. It was as if the words just flowed from my wrists of their own accord. I ran out of paper, so I used the napkins and backs of placemats from the food trays. Wherever there was space to write, I filled it with these words pouring from my soul. Day and night I felt this "need" to write, for it soothed my heart. I released all that was within me and stood naked in my soul and asked, *Who am I? What is my life's purpose now?* Then I waited for an answer.

By the fourth day after my diagnosis, April 11, 2006, I was starting to sense a shift in my perception of what life was now. I once again looked for the positive, for a lesson to be taken from the ordeal. Each small step within my mind gave me an ability to see past the pain, past the confusion, and I asked the Divine God for strength. One morning, I realized the answers to my soul-searching questions were what poured through my writing. Writing about my feelings and thoughts gave me strength to acknowledge them and then release them. That was a monumental shift, one that even my husband, Terry, felt and witnessed firsthand.

I remember his visit to my room, his kiss on my cheek. I smiled. His comment seemed confusing to me. "Welcome back", he said. And then I learned that the past three days I had been distant and too quiet, almost as if I were in another world. I could not even remember his visits, only my own depths of despair. But now, even though I still felt all those dark things, I was also able to feel the flicker of light within me that I called faith, hope, spirit, and soul. In that complete breakdown and release, I felt the quivering start of an awakening. Soon it would start to light up my days and grow. I again felt that North Star shining bright and high in the night's sky, lighting up the darkness, and I knew I must follow it. This light guided me without words, but with a deep sense of *knowing*.

Love and compassion heal wounded hearts whether it's from nurses you barely know, colleagues, friends, or family. I was aware that it never mattered where it came from, only that it came, and I hung on to it for dear life. Those who stepped forwards with their unconditional love, hope, and understanding helped me balance on the tightrope I walked upon. They were my heroes. On days when I thought, *What is the point of my life now?* these earthly angels allowed me to get beyond my own difficulties, my own mental pain, by taking charge and helping my family, which gave me time to adjust, to heal, and to learn how to live again, even with MS.

Teachers at my children's school went above and beyond the call of duty to help my children cope with the sudden change of their mother at the hospital. Courtney's grade-six teacher, Mrs. Veld, gave her own personal time to go to Courtney's horseback riding competition. She knew Courtney struggled with not having her mother there at her side, as I normally would have been. Mrs. Veld surprised Courtney at the barn. That act of compassion and kindness from her teacher was one of the greatest moments in Courtney's life. Someone she respected and loved had reached out to her and let her know she was not alone. There was also extra help with homework, counseling, and support available to our children to help them cope with the drastic changes within our family structure. Parents of schoolmates helped, too, by driving Courtney and Ainsley to and from their riding lessons.

It was an amazing feeling to know that support was there to help us get through the challenges while I was still hospitalized. As these friends shared their strength and compassion, I realized I was not alone in that battle at least. Terry had to return to his nightly shift work, so Bill, a close family friend for many years came to our rescue. He would stay overnight at our home, looking after the children, while Terry worked. Then he would leave once Terry had returned home. He loved the children and they loved him. His unconditional support allowed our kids to keep their regular home routines. That gave me peace of mind. Without him, I have no idea how we would have managed. I will be forever grateful that he stepped forwards to help us when we needed it most.

Two other dear friends, Pam and Irma, already anchors in my life, visited me in the hospital as much as they could. Pam and I had worked together, though in different departments. When she came on board, we quickly realized we had much in common. She too was a writer and had in fact published work. But it was more than that similarity that pulled us together. It felt as if we had known each other all our lives. We clicked; our friendship blossomed quickly and deeply almost of its own accord. Irma, too, I had met at work; she was an independent coach and consultant. Her teachings helped me to understand my own inner barriers, improving my abilities as a manager and leader, but also as a human being. Both friends took it upon themselves to fuel my understanding of what this disease was capable of and, more importantly, of what *I* was capable of.

Pam, gave me a huge white binder filled with what must have been every ounce of information on MS she could find, along with Web sites, organizations, and agencies that could help me. That binder became a permanent part of my taking charge of myself and my own healing, by learning all I possibly could about progressive multiple sclerosis. As I have little short-term memory retention, that binder was—and continues to be—a valuable tool in managing ever-changing information and options available to me.

Irma also walks her life with progressive MS. Her love and guidance helped me see beyond the confines of a disease that attacks my own cells. She helped me see change and challenges as gifts for the heart and soul, no matter if they came from a crippling disease that has no cure.

From all these acts of kindness, I pulled strength, and in that strength, I felt hope surfacing. Hope for a good life with my family and loved ones, hope for a life of meaning and contribution. I cannot stress enough how much the kindness of others helped pull me through the dark tunnel I was walking through. Their love lit lights in that tunnel, making me believe the end of it was always near. That gave me time to find my own strength again. I will be eternally grateful for all they gave.

On April 11, 2006, sixteen days after my admission to the hospital, I was to be transferred to the fourth floor. I said my good-byes to the staff on the third floor. I have never been hugged and loved by so many that I never really knew. I loved those nurses like family for, as they cared for me, I had grown to care for them, and I told them so. It had been a very special time for both the nurses and me. Friendship doesn't have to be forever in person, only forever in spirit.

The fourth floor was the rehabilitation unit for physiotherapy and care for slow, joint recovery. Most of the patients on this floor were seventy years and older—way older. Many had had hip replacements and looked at me rather strangely as I was transported into my new room. I felt like a toddler. Then I saw that most of them could get around the ward a lot faster than I could. How annoying that was to me!

The noise level on this floor made my ears ache even with earplugs. Everyone, including the nurses, seemed to be yelling constantly; call buttons rang nonstop; and if that didn't get the nurse's attention, there were a few patients who would just scream "Nurse!" so many times I wanted to go in there myself, and impersonate one just to make it stop. I hoped all this wouldn't trigger a setback. As I thought; *I am going to be positive, I am going to be positive!.*

As I settled into my new room, I did have to laugh when the new nurse, clipboard in hand, rattled off her list of questions without even looking at me. "Do you have all your own teeth? Do you wear dentures? Would you like your food pureed"? Her eyes widened in dismay as I shrieked, "I'm only forty"! She was most apologetic. Nonetheless, guess what showed up for my next day's meals … that's right, pureed goop!

I was not, of course, alone in my room, and the patient next to me drove me to distraction. My sheer exhaustion kept me in bed most of the time, yet she was awake at midnight blasting her television and keeping everyone awake. Her television was so loud I was sure they could hear it down on the third floor from where I had come. She refused to wear a headset because she said it hurt her head and messed her hair! Not only that, but she maintained a running dialogue with either herself or someone I couldn't see a good bit of the time. And I thought *I* was going insane! She told me she was "eighty-five years young"! She kept insisting I tell her which hip I'd had done. This was hard, because it was still difficult for me to say the words aloud, "I have MS". Finally, I did explain, and she was quiet for all of two minutes, taking it in, I supposed. Then she asked me, "Is that the left hip or the right hip?"

Not wanting to put myself through the whole ordeal again, I just mumbled, "The right".

"Oh, I knew that", she said.

Energy was not something I had in excess, and soon I knew I was indeed in trouble again—all these little things drained energy from me. I thought I had already pulled myself out of the depression that followed my diagnosis, but these seemingly little annoyances—constant noise being the primary one—dragged me back into it. The migraines returned and joined in with the existing neurological pain pounding in me. I struggled to maintain some inner peace. I needed it to heal and to plan my next move for recovery. My stress level climbed. Light was once again painful for my eyes. I could have sworn daggers were being stabbed into my skull as it exploded and shot electrical currents down my right side, ending in the feeling that my foot was engulfed in flames. I wanted to curl up into that all-too-familiar ball and die.

The nurses told me the rehab units on the fifth and sixth floors were better equipped for patients with neurological damage, geared to help stroke and other brain-injured patients, including people like me with multiple sclerosis. Unfortunately, those floors were quarantined because of the Norwalk virus! That virus was threatening to spread throughout the hospital, so visiting hours elsewhere were also now limited as a precaution. Terry found out from a posting on the door as he entered the hospital. It would be at least a week before I could transfer (*Oh no, not another blasted transfer*) to the sixth floor.

Once there, the doctor said it would take two to three weeks of heavy physiotherapy to learn to walk and use my right arm again, as well as train my left hand to compensate when needed. I would also receive help for my speech on the proper rehab floor. Everything was designed to retrain the knowledge that had been lost or gotten mixed up and jumbled in the mind. But first, I had to get some feeling back, some awareness of my body and mind. *If* and *when* that happened, I would face grueling lessons to relearn all that I had lost. I started to hate the word *if*. It presented too many paths when all I wanted was one—to get whole again.

In the meantime, the fourth-floor noise level was agony. My roommate, the one who chattered endlessly with invisible company as well as me, complained to someone on her phone (rather loudly, I might add) that I was unsociable! It brought me to tears. I was already confused enough and felt powerlessness to get anyone to understand. My speech issues compounded my physical agony. I thought my heart would explode from the pain her words inflicted.

I finally asked the nurse to help me explain my situation and to ask the woman to stop her abusive tirades, for I could not get the right words to come out my mouth. I thought relief and peace would set in. It lasted a stormy ten minutes. Now she complained to her invisible companion that I was rude and obnoxious because I had the bed next to the window!

Some patients seemed to not fully understand the idea of respect, much less gratitude. She was equally rude to all the nurses. Everyone, nurses and patients alike, were well aware of her lists of wants and needs. She made the nurses run off their feet for next to nothing. But I never once heard this miserable, spoiled old prune say thank-you to anyone. Nevertheless, demanding and ever irritable as she was, she too was my blessing. She showed me an aspect of human behaviour I did not want to be a part of. I did not want to be only a miserable taker; it was important for me to also have gratitude for the many blessings in my life, to give back to society, and to lead with a positive and passionate life force, no matter my challenges. And she was certainly a challenge.

I prayed long and hard to give me strength through those hours and days on that floor, while my neighbour squawked at me to get her a nurse. She wanted my call button, as well as her own. "To make the nurse come quicker!" she insisted. She was thirsty and wanted some juice! I knew she was troubled and did not intend to hurt with her words. But the feelings that raged inside me were too raw and volcanic. In some ways, she was acting out the anguish I felt deep inside me. Inner fear was taking its toll on me; I could sway from stable to unstable very quickly and didn't want to take it out on her or the nurses or anyone else. But I was in at least as much trouble as she—we had both lost our ability to control our own lives. Who could have a normal conversation about needing juice while all that was going on in their heads? I certainly could not! Talking continued to be difficult. I could sound like a drunken idiot and that was embarrassing enough. Moreover, it continued to be frustrating to have to try so hard to get the words to come out of my mouth properly, repeatedly I withdrew into silence. Adding to all my other fears, now I feared talking and sounding nuts … like this crazy patient next to me!

Then there were the lovely bodily functions from my new roommates that happened quite freely and regularly day and night—loud enough to wake me up and probably everyone on the upper and lower floors too. I had had enough. I was impatient with myself and wanted to go home. I figured if I had to listen to rip roaring bodily functions at all hours of the night, at least they ought to belong to my own family! Somehow that's easier to bear, although I am not sure why. All I remember thinking was that it was just too much information for me. I did not want to know what happened when you got old. I'd figure it out when I got there.

I had been desperately trying to keep my spirits high, but I was not winning while on this ward. Nothing was sacred anymore! One time, a nurse wheeled me into the very spacious washroom and transferred me to the commode to wait for Mother Nature to take over. She then left me alone, saying she'd come back to get me in a few minutes. Suddenly, the door swung open and I was staring at an older gentleman trying to get his wife (the patient) into the bathroom. We locked eyes for a few moments; I was sure I would faint!

He mumbled, "Let me know when you're done", like it was no big deal.

I looked at the gigantic mirror in front of me and said right out loud, "This can't be happening to me!" And then, to myself: *And who the heck wants to look into a gigantic mirror*—and I mean wall-to-wall gigantic—*while you are on the toilet in the first place?* I couldn't help myself; I was at the end of my rope, so it popped out, "Hello! Who designed this place?" The nurse popped her head around the door; as she looked at me, I could tell she was questioning my sanity. Never mind, so was I.

Of course I was scared of what my future held. And being with those dear souls who needed full care forced me to realize that I needed full care. And I didn't want it. I was a very independent and strong-willed woman. But MS stripped me of who I was, and at the time, I did not know who I would be or how to cope with that loss. I certainly did not want mirrors around me so I could see the useless body I had become.

I understood I needed to try to find my own inner healing and balance again. I had lost everything that I thought made me who I was. What was left was a shallow flicker of light within me, an inkling from my soul that no matter what the disease MS was doing to my mind and body, it could not touch the spirit that was my true essence. I needed to believe in me. I needed to assert to others what I needed for some inner healing and inner peace. So that, in time, though I would continue to have challenges with the disease, I could still have a life of meaning. To be a positive contributor to our world to the best of my ability was important to me. Therefore I needed to start the process of taking charge of my own healing ... again.

PART 2

Finding Hope and Inspiration

It's easiest to live with faith in the comforts of one's successes,
but hardest of all to keep faith through the suffering
that can accompany us as we journey through life.
How we cope with the latter, however,
shows our authentic light and soul to the world.
To accept and have faith in the Divine power deep within us,
to always see His light even when we may be crawling in darkness,
expands not only our faith, but also the universal faith of All

~Maureen Philpott Napier~
2008

CHAPTER 5

The Recovery

April 2006. It seemed like forever before the tears dried up. Before I could taste food again (using the term "food" loosely in reference to hospital meals), but it did happen. Although the ache and uncertainty stayed within my heart, I started to move on. But I also needed to release the emotional baggage that had built up from the dual trauma of my body's collapse and the subsequent changes to my life because of MS. Guilt, fear, deep sorrow, anguish, and a slew of other emotions sprouted like newly planted seeds. I called them my emotional weeds and set about imagining that I was pulling them up by their roots and tossing them out the window. *Look out below ... lest they fall on your head!*

Acknowledging that I could only do small tasks was another key step in my recovery. I was determined to push through the fog, but my words got all mixed up when I tried to talk, and I forgot much of the information I tried to read. The mental frustration was as draining as the physical side of MS. I had to slow down and be patient with myself in the days ahead as I tried to move on.

Though my life was now in upheaval, with anxiety and exhaustion hitting hard, I still kept trying to do more, heal fast, figure it all out, and get going. I was busy, after all, and didn't have time for wasting away in a hospital bed! But I couldn't figure it out. Nothing I tried worked. With my first treatment in physiotherapy, I learned quickly the extent of pushing beyond what the neurological abilities of my body were.

With therapists on either side of me, I was positioned inside a special, vertical walker that held me up. All I had to do was try to take a few steps. I fought with my mind to tell my right leg to move forwards, to take a step. It never responded. Not even a twitch. I tried to lean my weight into the walker to force my right leg to swing forwards, but I had no strength to stop myself from falling. As I crashed to the floor, my right leg went into spasms, and I almost passed out from the pain. By the time I was back in my bed, I was exhausted and slept for hours. I hadn't even taken one step. The fatigue associated with MS is grueling; it seeps deep beyond muscle and bone. Bringing with it an exhaustion you cannot fight against, as if even breathing and blinking take more energy than you feel you have.

Remember, the side that had lost function was my dominant side. I was right-handed, right-legged, right-footed! To put that in prospective, when you walk, you naturally start on your dominant side, and thus my right leg would have been the first leg to move forwards when walking. However, since my right side was numb, I had to try to get my *left* side to take over and become dominant. I had to teach the left side to become my anchor. That would allow me to move first with my left leg and then … drag … my right leg up to it. That may seem rather an easy thing to do. But with my brain damage (the *left* brain controls the right side of the body, the right brain, the left side of the body; I had brain damage on the left), I was also struggling to work with my left hand, so I could learn to write and feed myself properly. That training took time—a *lot* of time—and repetitive practice—repeating it over and over and over again.

On my second attempt with the therapists, I had a plan. In my mind, I repeated *left leg, right leg, left leg, right leg* over and over until, after much exertion, I took one step. The therapists rejoiced, but I wanted more, so I tried another step. The therapists told me not to overdo it, but, still in a hurry, I thought I could push the retraining. I tried to do one more step. I did not comprehend the learning curve, the effects of pushing myself, or the consequences I would face. I ended up pushing beyond what the neurological damage could handle. What a lesson. Because I tried to hurry to the finish line, I could not move at all for the remainder of that day and night. I suffered extreme pain in my right leg, which again felt as if my foot was in a burning pit of fire.

As the physiotherapist explained to me the differences between neurological damage compared to, say, damage from a broken leg, I started to understand that I needed to make a 180-degree shift in my thinking. Previously, with my martial arts training, I pushed through the pain, pushed through what my body was telling me were my limits. I created new limits each time, pushing the boundaries of what I could do. That type of thinking was what drove me now to do more, but with neurological damage, that type of thinking slows your recovery to almost nil. At first, I did not accept their explanations; it didn't jibe with how I had lived my life prior to these setbacks. I always pushed my boundaries, personally and professionally. Limitations were a weakness I had never allowed myself to have. I needed to change that mindset before I could see any continual improvement in my healing.

> Bring forth the poisons of the false self and, as you release the pain and suffering, you *will* heal. To leave the poisons within you will destroy you—for as they fester, their power grows, and the light of your soul diminishes.
>
> ~Maureen Philpott Napier~
> 2008

My mind played tricks on me; the driven perfectionist within was driving me insane. *Perfectionists cannot hit rock bottom, there is too much to do, not enough time, and no one else to do it the right way!* The painful agony of not being able to control my own body, my own mind, and my own life was reflected in such self-torture. I was not able to do what I had always done. I couldn't "just do it". The depth of that realization hit me hard, leading me down an all-new path of panic, anxiety, and depression. This time, for failing (which I hadn't done yet, but never mind), it did little to ease my pains. It took time for me to understand that a perfectionist, a driven overachiever constantly on the go, always in control, always striving for the next goal, the next task, the next success, would not do. I could no longer be that. And it was okay to ask for help. I had not failed. *But how would my life be now?* I wondered. *How would I contribute to my family?* I worried. *Would my career still be anything I had hoped and planned for? Where was my life's journey heading to now?* I had to take a deep and honest look inside myself and ask, *Who am I* and *what do I truly need to feel whole again?* I had to stop looking and forecasting my future and just live moment to moment. I could not worry about my future—I had to be present in the current moment, now. And heal now.

The echo of the woman I had been taunted me; she seemed so far away. I wondered if I would ever be her again. As the hours rolled on— and the sweat rolled down—it would be through therapy, I knew that the perfectionist within me had to end. My body had new parameters of what it could and could not do. I needed to acknowledge that, surrender to it, and stop judging myself for my external accomplishments. That was insane and it had to stop. *(Did I just say that?)* My identity had been tied up in everything external to myself: mother, wife, research scientist, friend, daughter, sister, even a foe. I *was* my accomplishments, as well as my failures in life; even my unfinished, but well-planned, future was my identity. All these external titles and roles were who I thought I was. But as these became more and more remote, my writing gave me a different outlook. I sensed something greater than myself—but that I was a part of—blossoming within me, tempting me like a forbidden fruit high up in the apple trees.

This was not a quick change in thought, though. It was a slow, laboured trek up a bloody mountain. As I worked with the therapists, there were many more failures than wins—and neither was clearly one or the other. Each time I fell, each time my blasted leg stood still as a tree trunk or my arm lay motionless by my side, I found strength and determination to accept that at that moment, it did not want to move. I accepted it; it was okay; I was okay. Each time that I *did* make it move, I endured spasms and excruciating pains down the right side of my body. But I would give thanks for the movement, no matter the pain I had to endure. Each failure brought acceptance, a win of a new kind. Each win, brought pain, but gratitude and forgiveness for the failures.

Fear and Me

When doubt knocks on your heart's door
It is frightening to open and let in
The thoughts that swirl within your head
The demons of the unsaid

Yet if we take the step ahead
Breathing through the fear instead
We may find the answers
Waiting on the other side
Within the cathedral of our souls

For in fear resides your escape
But one must look deep within
And let fear know it has no grip
Or power over your heart and soul

To move on, look fear squarely in its eye
Have faith and hope from the Divine that ties
You and our Beloved as One
Then your fear will finally be gone

Maureen Philpott Napier
April 28, 2006

CHAPTER 6

Accepting What Is

I continued to write. My silent words on paper did not seem as backwards as they did in verbal discussions. I was able to release in these written words, my thoughts, my tears, and my aches ... and give them away. The process also enabled me to see the beauty around me and within me. Slowly, I started to notice my life moving forwards more positively. In one moment of inner clarity, I acknowledged that the past was in the past and the future was still (and always would be) in the future.

As I continued with my writing, I could sense the shift within myself: to live *in the present moment,* the one we have right here, right now. Understanding that helped take the bricks off my back, so to speak, so I could deal with only the present moment of *now.* But it would be a repetitive realization, a brick-by-brick effort to remove old thought patterns and habitual behaviours and replace them with the wings of a new perspective. It took repetitive and deliberate conscious thought, plus the element of time in the healing process.

I had my diagnosis of MS. Now it was a matter of understanding MS, living with MS, and healing with MS. I needed patience and compassion for myself—probably my hardest lesson of all—and I needed to let go of the former map of my life, to finally accept the new path before me. What would be, would be.

Part of the confusion going on in my mind had to do with the capabilities and functions of the left hemisphere of the brain as compared to the right hemisphere of the brain. It might have helped if I had understood that at the time, but there was no one to explain those differences to me. It could have relieved much confusion and anxiety.

As I described before, the left hemisphere of the brain controls the right side of your body and the right hemisphere of your brain controls the left side of your body. As I was admitted to the hospital, there were actually two different incidents going on. First, I was having a severe migraine attack affecting the right hemisphere of my brain and the right side of my face. Second, I was having an undiagnosed MS attack in the left hemisphere of my brain that was paralyzing the right side of my body (right arm, torso, and leg.) The neurological trauma affecting my left hemisphere affected my thought processes, which caused my language and, at times, my memory to behave completely askew.

As the damage surfaced, the trauma left me floundering, as if I were completely lost. That happened because the neuropathways within my left hemisphere were incapable of completing the circuits needed for thought processes, including my language, my patchwork quilt of memories that made up my life, in short, my identity. Auditory information was received sporadically as the neurological malfunction took hold of the left hemisphere of my brain. At the time, I fought hard to regain control of my thoughts, but I understood neither what was happening in my mind, nor the effect of damage on the shifting between the hemispheres. As the neurological trauma on my left hemisphere increased, the right hemisphere started to come forwards and help the brain relay information to the rest of my body. Eventually, through retraining and what I called remapping of my brain, it would become the more dominant hemisphere.

All the research and reading I did led me to understand the basic workings of the right hemisphere (see the Appendix at the end of the book for a list of Web sites, CDs, and books that helped me heal in body, mind, heart, and soul). As a scientist, I found the knowledge not only fascinating, but also invigorating. I was like a child learning everything anew. I saw how the right hemisphere was filled with my spirituality, my creativity, and even my ability to connect to the whole

Universe as *One*. The right brain only cares about the present moment, and so how much time something took was completely irrelevant to it. The opening up of my right brain brought me to the understanding that there is no separation between humans, nature, animals, air, water, planets, and thus the universe: *All is One*. It gave me the spiritual warmth, the expansiveness surrounding love, compassion, and thus emotional well being and inner peace that I was desperate for. It showed me the vast, limitless, and empowering connection to the universal source that I call God, but that has been given many different names in many different forms of religion and spirituality. The concept that *We Are All One* repeatedly floated into my mind, and it brought me strength. As I periodically started to contemplate the meaning behind those words, I would sense a comforting peace within the confusion.

Parts within my brain continued to shut down from the neurological malfunctions within the left hemisphere. But my right hemisphere opened a door that I had never before been aware I even had. It would lead me through the pain and inner self-torture of failure, guilt, and confusion. What had previously shaped my sense of self-worth was forever changed, and I started to recognize that new understanding within myself. My soul's evolution was forever changing and unfolding throughout the healing journey through MS.

I had to look at all my equipment and supplies, including my wheelchairs, not as burdens, but as tools I used to live more freely. I started to laugh at the crazy stuff my body did—and did not—do. I was not a sinking ship—I was a canoe with no paddles! I knew I had the determination it took to move forwards into the light that shines brightly for all of us … as long as I didn't give up. That would become another huge step forwards in my inner healing: Love myself as I Am, even with a progressively destructive form of MS. Days went by one by one. My resolve to tackle one moment at a time and to not run too quickly into the future helped control the exhaustion and the fogginess within my brain.

The neurological effects on my left hemisphere seemed to sporadically turn off and on. As if the neurons were trying to get the signals through the damaged areas of my brain. As if a light switch was repeatedly being flicked on and off. Therefore old thought patterns and behaviours would spontaneously resurface at times, causing me to want to rush headlong "back to normal". In those moments, I denied that MS would have any hold on me. After all, if you just put your mind to it, you can do anything, right? Wrong again! Sometimes that's not the lesson. As I struggled against my paralysis and concentrated on coping with new equipment that was supposed to ease the strain, I was unknowingly slowing my recovery. The more I pushed myself, the worse things got. I was learning the hard way how tight a hold MS had on me. Complete exhaustion resulted very quickly if I pushed myself too hard. Letting go of those old behavioural instincts and patterns would be an ongoing challenge for some time. I started by trying to redirect the pushing habit by looking harder into myself to understand the lessons being presented and find new answers there. If I couldn't learn from these lessons, how could I possibly be able to move through my journey with MS?

I had to learn to guard my energy reserves by becoming aware of early signs of fatigue, such as spasm and pain spikes. To ignore these signs meant days of immobility, excruciating pain, and mental confusion. I had to learn to concentrate on only one thing at a time or my brain would short-circuit and the confusion would escalate. I could no longer multitask. I could not walk with the hospital walker and talk to someone at the same time. If I was concentrating on getting my right leg to step forwards and someone called my name, distracting me, I would fall. On good days, physiotherapy exercised my motor skills and speech therapy my language and thinking skills. On a great day, my left arm got my food into my mouth without spilling it! Fatigue consumed me and I would sleep for hours even after little tasks. Each task and every lesson drained me completely. The exhaustion was beyond anything I had ever experienced. I would melt into the bed and fade to nothing.

When I was awake, I took full advantage of my sense of humor. And plenty happened that was laughable: My right leg flopping out of bed on its own, unbeknownst to me. Trying to sit up by myself without falling to one side and getting literally stuck between pillows and bedrails, and then needing to be rescued. Being unable to open the packages on my food tray—what a relief! Wasn't that wallpaper paste that kept showing up for breakfast? *Oh, it's oatmeal.*

Little did my nurses know, my rather robust roommate got most of my food—she was always starving. For me, eating was another chore. I had to force myself to consume food; it was so draining to even chew. Of course, the physical signals that normally let you know you are hungry were not working either, so I had no sense of it, no hunger pains. Consequently, it was quite easy to miss a meal. Also, swallowing food and then digesting it was not only difficult, but painful. I was a complete bloody mess! Somehow I managed to keep the laughter alive any way I could—how my inability to digest the hospital food without feeling like I was about to throw up could strike me as funny, I don't know. But I used it.

There were always opportunities to laugh. My friend Jim, who was in for respiratory care, and I had some good discussions that either raised our eyebrows in astonishment, or had us laughing uncontrollably. I would ask him what he got for lunch; his facial expression of gagging was enough to alert me he got what I got. We shared so much laughter, poking fun at how bad the food was. Something as silly and comical as that was able to remove the heartache of our pain. He would then venture forth to the onsite Tim Hortons and get us a couple of coffees with donuts. (His legs worked, mine did not)

Jim was a kindred soul that kept my spirits high. Maybe the sugar had something to do with it too, but either way as we shared our coffees we shared not only our pain but also our strength.

More than just a survival technique, humor turned out to be my bridge. It was the beginning of what would become a greater consciousness of my heart and soul on a spiritual level, which I had never previously felt. Does it seem strange that deep suffering from an illness or disease is what opens that awareness? Perhaps it must be that way. I never would have met Jim and his wife, Miriam, if we were not in the hospital—they are both enjoying retirement now and, therefore, at a different stage in life than I am. Our paths crossed because of illness and shared sadness and humor. These brought the gift of friendship, a mutual gift of loving and caring for someone else. We had some good laughs, Jim and I. That got me through some choppy waves of heart-wrenching emotion. Then again, maybe it was the sugar!

In the early stages of knowing I had MS, my visitors brought me their love, their strength, and their compassion. As I lay on the hospital bed, I was obviously not myself. I was still mentally weak, confused, and physically fatigued. I was literally crippled into a slumber of semi-awareness. Yet my visitors' soft touch and soothing words could bring me back into conscious reality. They would sit with me in silence, but speak volumes. They looked past the effects that the disease had caused, and I understood they still loved me.

My friends, my husband, and even some nurses would come to sit with me and, though I could not feel my body, I could feel the sharing of love, and my weakness seemed to diminish. I could sense myself responding to their warmth, their selfless love, and their compassion. It helped me understand that no matter what level or kind of love they shared, it was deeply affecting my healing. This understanding presented the most valuable message I received in those early days of pain and terror. I sensed their soothing touch as they stroked my hand. The gentle whispers of their commitment to help me heal. The chapters of my favourite authors that they read, and the angel stones they placed by my bed. The abundance of flowers that brightened my room with fragrant blossoms. The angel figurine that watched over me day and night. The attentive nurse who gentled her touch as she washed my hair, realizing the activity hurt my head dreadfully, and then talked to me to distract me from the remaining pain. Now I know the right hemisphere of my brain was the part of me that both craved and experienced that connection, peace, and love from friendly others. And with these connections, I thrived. My strength grew from their commitment to love me.

While the neurological trauma to my left hemisphere diminished my awareness of what was going on around me, my right hemisphere stabilized my sense of the present moment by being able to experience the inner peace, love, and ever-flowing warmth that my visitors shared with me. They may not have even been aware of how significant their actions were to me. But I was fully aware of how their actions made me feel. I felt loved! No matter what they saw with their eyes or heard with their ears, they still loved me. They loved the essence of who *I Am*. I could feel how they were part of me and how I was part of them. That gave me a special strength that I could lean on.

Many nights, I waited in anticipation for them to come see me. It kept me connected to the outside world, and I needed the injections of love and warmth they offered me. Even with the ongoing despair, their visits could often refuel me, letting me see, through them, that my own strength, compassion, and love were still intact. Inner awareness and inner healing began bit by bit because of these experiences. I needed to be surrounded with positive energy from my visitors, rather than harangued by someone who rambled on, complaining about all that was wrong in the world and their surroundings. Ahem, like my roommate.

My *left* hemisphere's damage continued to cause me difficulty processing what I was hearing at times; people spoke far too fast for me to comprehend. I needed them to slow down and often repeat their sentences, so I could grasp what they were saying. But even then, I was often out of touch. My right hemisphere, as described earlier, had surfaced to try to help get signals through my brain to my body. (Remapping, recreating my brains electrical pathways.) I was more aware of the "feeling" side of me than usual, and these feelings were more exaggerated than usual. So, I responded very well to warm, or positive, feelings and styles that others offered me. They helped me get "outside of myself". I could watch them and how they interacted. I was in awe of their love as they shared it with me, and my sense of well being resonated within my very soul.

I was even sensitive to the differences within the hospital staff. Some would take an extra moment to smile or otherwise acknowledge my presence: a touch on my shoulder, a pat on my leg. But to others, I seemed only to be a number, a nameless brain-injured patient that filled a bed. The harsh or abrupt movements and comments these staff members used confused me. I did not understand them, but neither could I put words together to express how they were affecting me. Incoming sound and light had still been painful, and I recoiled from it. Patients in my condition should be treated like infants or very small children—sudden movements or angry loud voices will startle them and they cry until soothed. The damage to my left hemisphere returned me in some way to that childlike uncertainty about what was going on all around me. Other people could aggravate that vulnerability into emotional and physical agony or soothe it completely into something Divine.

The right hemisphere of my brain allowed the feelings of oneness and inner peace to start to float within my conscious thoughts. My spirit, my soul, seemed to stretch out and breathe. I began to grow in mental strength and clarity and become more capable of handling the hurdles I faced with MS. All my right hemisphere's senses were hyperactivated, producing a feeling of wholeness within me, even though my body and mind (as I knew it) had crumbled.

Later on when I was alone, I began to be able to sense the differences between the hemispheres of my brain. When my left hemisphere "came on line", my thoughts were incisive, but often rigid and consumed in negative self-talk of hopelessness. When my right hemisphere came forwards, I felt peaceful warmth from my spirituality, a surging love *for All*, and a connection to the vast universe and those around me. It was that awareness that gave me a new way to look at life, enabling me to continue asking what my lessons were within all these challenges. I was able to seek a deeper understanding of who I was.

I knew I faced an uphill battle. The repeating challenges were many and steep, but I had always believed there were lessons to learn in every situation and that remaining positive was half the battle won. I again prayed while visualizing myself walking, surrounded in a wheat field with wild flowers, the bright blue sky and sun shining down upon me. I could hear the distant waves of the ocean crash ashore. That was a repetitive visualization I often used to soothe my heart and soul. It had worked well in past visualizations to calm me and root myself as a healthy whole person. I prayed for strength to face each lesson and learn from it, so that I could continue to grow and serve within the new path I would walk. Could I go on being the person I had been, different, yet in some way also the same? I felt as if the person I thought I was had died. In turn, a seed deep within me had started to grow, but it would need ongoing nourishment. A small spark of light from a lost part of my soul was born within the darkness that drained and devoured everything in its path. With that compassion, love, and understanding from those that surrounded me, I started to recreate myself and my new life with MS.

Accepting "what is" brought its own sense of wisdom and transformed me. As I searched deep within, an inner wisdom guided me to explore more of my heart and soul. Each stage within that healing brought a new awareness. Sometimes it brought pain, sorrow, and depression. Other times, it brought hope, happiness, and spiritual elation. I wanted to heal the despair, to be a beacon of hope and inspiration to those around me. If I could just dispel the negative suffering that at times consumed me and consciously choose to emit positive energy, then I knew I could live my life well with MS.

Stillness, Silence and Solitude's Renewal

For one to heal
Silence and stillness
Is not only desired
But Divinely required
As it was before time, it is again

Understand, it is only in the words not spoken
That the stillness of one's mind
Creates the abilities within
For a soul to heal
This you do not need to fear
Stillness is thy inner reflection
Silence allows thy own Divine whisper
To be heard
Acknowledge this power within
And with your trust and faith
Know without a shadow of a doubt
This healing time
Requires this silence and stillness of one's mind
To begin

Ideally one could remove thy body
To a heart and soul retreat
There, nature would encompass your soul
And together you would grow as friends do
Loved and strong
Faith and trust that you belong
Would be seeds planted
That would turn to full blooms before long
Yet if this retreat is impossible to do
Request from those close to you
The understanding of this time
For thy healing has already begun
The absolute need of this time
To heal and to rest

For it will help you find
Strength, love and inner power
This important grace
Found within, helps get you through another day
No matter how grim

His Divine intelligence
Beckons your essence to explore
The confines of mind, body, and soul
In the silence and stillness of one's mind
And also the rest of this body at this time
Opportunities surface for inner healing
Requesting space, requesting understanding
Of the surge within me that is calling me
To be in silence, to be in stillness
To be in solitude
He has spoken
I have heard, but it's still my choice
To commence with His directions
And the affirmations to heal
Or stay under the cloud of doom and fear

I choose to live and contemplate
The many calls, to me as whispers
Again and again
Now I listen closely for I have heard
It is time to heal and renew
Myself
In the stillness of mind
In the silence of the unheard
In the solitude I need not words

Maureen Philpott Napier
February 13, 2008

CHAPTER 7

Finding My Own Way

April 14, 2006. It had now been almost twenty-one days since my initial admission. I made a decision that was not well received by the nurses and rehab personnel that had been caring for me on the fourth floor. The previous night I had made up my mind: I wanted to go home and heal. I craved peace and quiet, and I was not getting that. I knew the staff and therapists rebutted my release for my own good. But I also knew I was sinking where I was. My only chance was to get home and try to get on with my life—whatever that was. With homecare, my family and friends around me, I knew I would be better off. That's not to say it would be easy, but it was my last hope for normality. As it turned out, fate was on my side. The Norwalk virus was still spreading through the hospital, which posed a higher risk to those of us with compromised immune systems.

My family doctor walked me through the pros and cons of hospital care versus homecare. But I was able to get across to him my difficulties on the fourth floor ward. He understood my migraines and thus understood how the ward's noise level was excruciating for me. Add to that my malfunctioning neurological response to the noise and light, and it was clearly not a good place for me to rest and heal. He finally agreed and signed my papers: I was to be released and granted homecare.

"How soon do you want to go home?" he asked me.

My answer was instant, "Immediately!"

He shook his head as he headed for the nurses' station and, laughing over his shoulder, said, "I'll see if I can get you home today!"

How I rejoiced at the possibility of going home. I knew I would see my children and have a chance to ease their pain, as well as the burden of everyone battling to keep our family's life normal while I was in hospital. That alone would ease my inner battle of guilt for failing them somehow.

The hospital agreed to release me only if I agreed to be transported home by ambulance and sign a waiver of liability if I fell or was injured. "I don't care if you stick me in a cannon and fire me off home", I responded, signing gladly with scribbles. I think the discharge nurse thought I was joking—I was not! She didn't have much of a sense of humor anyway!

Whatever was needed I was willing to do. When the ambulance crew came they got me onto their stretcher and strapped me on. Restraints across my chest, hips, knees and ankles held me in place. I felt a strange sensation leaving the hospital, totally aware *I had no control* over my body, and yet I was going out into the *real* world. The sun was shining so brightly I needed sunglasses. It was thrilling but also extremely painful for my eyes. As we left the hospital grounds, I asked the ambulance crew, two petite women, if they planned on parachuting me out of the ambulance when we got home; I could not fathom how these women were going to get me *into* my house. I laughed at my absurd situation. My mind repeatedly asked *Is this my life?* The paramedic chatted with me to distract me from my obvious pain, but the ride home was so bumpy I actually passed out a couple of times, horrendous pain overwhelming me. When I came to, she was holding my hand, assuring me I was okay. The restraints, after all, were a good idea. But couldn't they fill those blasted potholes quicker? Still, what a glorious day it was! So, I cursed the light; I cursed the roads; I cursed the bumps. But I was so excited to be heading home that I didn't really care about the pain. *But please God, no more pain!*

We drew closer to my home and I could not contain my happiness. The tears flowed, but this time, I cried tears of joy—I was home … almost! I wished I could walk up the stairs to my house like I had before or even just to make it easier on that ambulance crew trying to carry me up them. "Sorry for the bench press", I remarked as they transferred my weight onto the special chair that lifted me up the steep stairs. The medications I was on—good old steroids, used to quickly reduce the swelling on my brain and spine—had increased my weight by almost forty pounds! I was like an overstuffed rag doll, filled with wet cement, flopping all over the place with an extra forty pounds of dead weight (and if you think I am going to tell you my actual weight, your brain is inflicted with something other than common sense too)! It was exhausting for them, I could tell. But there was nothing I could do. I felt helpless. I *was* helpless.

I was a little worried they were going to drop me into my flowerbeds. Thank God they never checked my heart rate. I was a nervous wreck with visions of us all going down the stairs backwards! I shut my eyes tight, and prayed. Why couldn't they send two big guys to transport me? Firefighters would work, well never mind, that would also not have helped my erratic heartbeat! But those women were professional paramedics and they had a goal. They were determined, even through the huffing and puffing, to get me into the house and back on the stretcher.

Now the medics had the task of getting me into my bed. Except my bed was on wheels, and it moved every time they tried to plop me on it. Turns out, wheels are good for cleaning, but not so good when you're trying to put a dead weight wearing silk pajamas on the bed. I slipped off the edge as it wheeled away. Three grown adults, including my husband, had to tackle me onto the bed. Now I know what a football feels like in the middle of a scrimmage! I think they all thought I was insane—all I could do was laugh hysterically. Luckily for all of us, laughter can be contagious, and between my body doing its own thing, the bed moving its own way, and all of us laughing, we were quite a mess. I don't know if you'd call it a teaching moment, but it sure was a good healing laugh.

Note to self: no more silky pajamas!

April 14, 2006. By early afternoon, I was finally home and the uncertainty of the days ahead did not matter that much, for I was content with just living *now*. I felt an inner peace flowing from within me. Somehow being home was enough. I needed nothing else.

We had planned on surprising the children. They did not know I was coming home because my release happened very quickly once I was approved—bed space in the hospital was still at critical levels. I waited for them to come home from school, counting down the hours and the minutes as my heartbeat throbbed in anticipation. I had not let them come to the hospital too many times. I did not want them to see the pain on the wards, and with Norwalk threatening visitation times, I took to caution and talked to them mostly by phone, with occasional short visits.

Truth was, the pain I felt at having to be the way I was in front of my children had been emotionally traumatic not only for me, but also for them. Seeing what you see in hospitals can traumatize children, and I have probably overprotected them from the pain the world can bear. I wanted them to run and play in the new sunshine that spring brought to us and be what children should be: young, free, playful, and happy. Why should they see me like that? How would they cope—they were still so young? Moreover, how would I cope?

It didn't matter any longer. The moment arrived when Terry ushered them into my bedroom; like a train on tracks they followed one after the other. Courtney screamed; tears streamed down her face. She fell onto my bed, as if the uncontrollable tears shattered her inner strength. Ainsley was jumping up and down like a jack in the box, her screams so high-pitched I felt my head explode again. Though her tears were more controlled, I could see her body shaking; her legs seemed to want to collapse from underneath her. She appeared unable to stop the combination of jumping and shaking, as if her energy was coming out in ways she could not control. Terry picked her up and placed her on the bed beside me. She did not touch me but looked deep into my eyes. I understood her uncertainty. And lifted my arm to guide her to me; she burrowed into my chest and let the tears flow.

Alastair used his small hands and arms to wipe away his tears. He had streaks of dirt across his face, and I thought how handsome he was at that very moment as he gripped Terry's leg for stability. I heard him say, "But she's not fixed yet, Daddy". As he picked Alastair up to put him on the bed beside me, Terry replied, "No she's not fixed, but she loves you just the same". Alastair snuggled into me, his small arms wrapped so tightly around my neck it's a wonder I could still breathe.

I felt his tears and kisses through my pajamas. Something happened to my heart as if it became swollen, a sponge soaking up water, my family's love so pure it overflowed within me.

Terry and I looked at each other, our pain and awareness of our children's distress painfully displayed in our eyes. Sometimes I was in complete awe how we could communicate so deeply, but say nothing at all. Had twenty-one years of marriage, of friendship, of trials and tribulations as well as happiness and successes allowed us to see beyond the pain and anguish with compassion and forgiveness with a faith that no matter what we faced we would work it out? It was one of those timeless, precious moments where past heartaches seemed unimportant. It seemed to me as if time itself froze, and as I stared at my family, I made a silent pact with God. *I won't give up!* Their screams, tears, hugs, and kisses had renewed my soul. I was sure that very moment that whatever risks I took at being home, without hospital care, was worth it a million times over. From that day forwards, we became a *family dealing with MS,* and I knew in my heart that the love my children gave me would help both my husband and me get through the days ahead. One of the first things we did was to move my bed downstairs and the kids' upstairs. And we got rid of those wheels!

Since Terry worked nights he was able to maintain our children's evening routines with dinner, homework, baths—things I still couldn't do by myself, or even for myself. Then he left for his night shift. I had to accept, as painful as it was, that I could not physically care for our children. And probably wouldn't be able to for some time. I felt as if I had failed them as their mother.

Our friends came to help with the bedtime routines for the children (their bedrooms were upstairs). The children were used to having bedtime stories read to them, maybe a little tickle session as they were tucked into bed, along with their goodnight kisses. The change in their bedtime routine was hardest on Alastair and Ainsley. Alastair was just learning to read, and I was no longer able to read to him. Ainsley would ask me what a word was in her book, and I would look at it but not know the word or even be able to pronounce it. So, friends took over helping with bedtime routines. They stayed while the kids said goodnight to me downstairs and then tucked them in with bedtime stories, before saying goodnight themselves.

We had adjusted their routines and kept as much as we could the same. Thanks to Bill, Pam, and Irma, this worked well for all of us. Through Community Care Access Centre (CCAC), we had all the equipment I needed on loan for the first month home, until we bought our own equipment—wheelchairs, vertical standing walker, you name it—and help with meal preparation tasks like peeling potatoes, the use of occupational therapists, physiotherapists, and a speech therapist. Red Cross support looked after all my personal care and was also part of CCAC. My case manager within CCAC contacted the MS society to investigate if they had equipment in their loan cupboard that I could use, rather than my having to buy it right away. The dollar signs just kept climbing in our minds. I tried to redirect my focus to just living peacefully within my beautiful home.

My home seemed to have fallen into complete disarray in my absence. (Though, I was not surprised!) Terry and the kids thought it looked just fine! Terry slanted a sideways look in my direction as he proclaimed he had cleaned up prior to me getting home. I had smiled and nodded, but my mind silently whispered to me, *Really, where?* I could not live up to my previous expectations on how my home was maintained. The slightest mess or the smallest warren of dust bunnies left me frustrated like heck. Of course, I wanted to get up and go look after it, put our home back to clean and crisp, but I couldn't. Neither could I produce a special meal when my family needed a treat after I had an attack of perfectionism with chores and duties. My colleagues at work pitched in and gave us Molly Maid services and gift cards for restaurants that delivered. What a godsend! They understood I needed to feel like my family and our home were looked after. Within the first few weeks home, they gave me peace of mind with those gifts, and reduced much of my own inner anxiety regarding our home and meals. I am forever thankful for my colleagues' support and proud that I worked with such compassionate people.

I must confess, my brain still told me to get up and clean the house, for the cleaners were coming! My body, however, pointed out what I fool I was. For the first month, it was a challenge getting routines and setting standards to what was realistic sorted out, so that we could go on living as a family with limited stress, considering all the changes we were going through. I also had to revisit my own level of expectations versus the reality of the moment. The reality that I was unable to maintain my home as I previous had, versus the illusion that my family would have those same expectations as I had, and the house would again be *perfect. Ah, how many ways have I been a fool, I'm losing count!* But seriously, how can they think a hand towel scrunched into a ball and stuffed between wall and rack is the best way for the damn thing to dry in this millennium? I am not sure I really want the answers to those strange questions that pop into my head at odd moments. The gobs of toothpaste left in the sink are giving me a headache!

Every day brought a flurry of activities associated with helping me continue to heal at home. At first, there were three different support personnel working with me while I learned how to get from my bedroom to the bathroom to the living room and then to the kitchen by wheelchair or my special vertical walker. With these aids and aides, I was able to get up, around, and enjoy being home. Still, I was sleeping an enormous amount of time. Even after minor exertion, my body needed sleep to rejuvenate. Every day I would do as many of the physiotherapists' exercises as I could manage—if I could manage—enduring more and more pain to get myself towards walking and functioning again in some small part within my home. Then I would sleep, exhausted. Each little triumph, as I learned to use my unique vertical walker and my right arm, gave me a sign that I was moving in the right direction.

In the evening, each of my children turned into little nurses in their own ways. They too needed to feel helpful, like they were making a positive difference in my health and welfare. My six-year-old, Alastair, loved to check my heart, to make sure it was still "clicking". He had seen one of the nurses at the hospital pick up my hand to check my heart rate, so that's how he did it, checking the *back* of my hand, no matter what I told him. Eight-year-old Ainsley wanted to know all the sore spots on my body and when they were going to get better. Perhaps I needed a special, Barbie Band-Aid? And my favourite, did I want some of *her* chocolate? Courtney, a grown-up eleven, understood the severity of my issues better than the other two. Possibly a might burdened, she was quiet and reserved, at times taking charge of the situation by reminding the others, "Mum needs to rest". Then she would scoot them all out the door to give me a bit of peace and quiet. Within minutes, I would fall fast asleep, as if I hadn't slept in days.

I could have said *no* to their help. I could have said, "You're doing it the wrong way"; I could have said, "I am in too much pain and too exhausted for this". But they were sharing their love and compassion with me, and I openly welcomed it, no matter what they felt I needed, and I thanked them for their wonderful care. Their smiles would beam at my appreciation, and I could see they were thriving, no matter the challenges we all faced.

It took some time for them to take it in that I was home to stay. At first, they would repeatedly open my door just to check that I was indeed still in my bed resting. Once rested, they would come back in and make a commotion fussing over me. Fluffing my pillows and propping them up behind me, so that I could lean back and enjoy periods with each one reading me stories. That was the time I loved the most. When they read to me, it was as if I were watching a live performance, with all their mannerisms and voice changes. I fought hard not to giggle, grab them up, squeeze them tight, and smother them with kisses! Is that just a mother thing?

Alastair was happy to sit by my side, rubbing my arm and my leg. He would ask if I needed an extra hug and kiss for my "booboos". Of course, my answer was always yes. He would climb up on my bed, snuggling into my side, and ask, "When are you going to be better, Mummy?" It was the hardest thing to admit that I did not know, but the honest truth was also the most healing for me. Being open and honest with my family allowed us all to understand the disease a little better. The effects of MS were not easy to hide; they were extreme and severe. Our children could not help but see me and the disease's effects on me, but they also knew that I kept a positive attitude and tried not to dwell on the negatives. They would frequently roll their eyes when I would say, "Quick, think of something positive!" (Their brains worked faster than mine).

The two older girls took on the task of running the household. They came in my room one afternoon wearing headscarves and the kitchen aprons we used when baking. *I Love Lucy* flashed in my mind! I guess playing house all those times had paid off. Courtney was in charge, with little sister Ainsley trying hard to show me she was big too. At one point, Courtney walked into my room and declared, "I don't know where my time goes, there is just *too* much to do!" Ainsley added, "Me too". I wanted to laugh or sympathize, but before I could get a word out of my mouth, they had turned and promptly headed back to the kitchen. I rolled my eyes, without really realizing that Alastair was watching. He shrugged his shoulders and said, "Girls", like that described the whole situation perfectly. But I was actually thinking, *Holy crap, they were listening to me all those times!* I sure knew the feeling. Somehow, these moments let me know that some things had not changed in my life.

For the next couple of weeks, my children took turns having nights with Mum. Normally I would have insisted they slept in their own beds. Rules were rules (unless they had a fever), or some other illness I needed to keep an eye on. That was before MS entered my life and forced me to realize what was truly important. But now, as each asked for their turn to sleep with me and take care of me while Terry worked, those old rules were broken. They wanted to make sure I was okay through the night, and they were great helpers. Roles seemed reversed as they would cuddle up to me on my bed and read me stories. Alastair read from the pictures, and I found I did the same thing. Words were still hard for me to verbally release. Ainsley taught me the words in her book, almost as if she were the teacher and I the student. I learned slowly, but with time, their love and guidance, I did start to relearn much of my lost vocabulary.

They helped me wash my face—with a face cloth that was much too wet—and then dry it—with a towel also much too wet! The girls brought my toothbrush and cup to me, and I tried to use my left hand to brush my teeth. It was a messy experience. I was still training my left hand to take over what my right hand had always done, but could no longer. Alastair frowned at the difficulties I was having and reminded me, "You have to brush really well; it's a rule". I continued for a few more moments and then called it quits, exhausted. Taking pity on me, Alastair commented, "Mummy, you are already old; maybe you don't need your teeth anymore", thinking he had it all figured out. Ouch! But too fatigued to worry about my blasted teeth or my age, I leaned back against my pillows, and he read me more stories and tucked me in for the night with a kiss on my forehead. By the end of the second month, the children were looking after their own bedtime routines with Courtney's leadership, so family life began to normalize.

I was awake a fair amount through the night because of pain and leg spasms. But it was also one of my more emotionally healing, loving, peaceful times, because I was able to watch each of my little nurses, as they slept beside me. In those moments, they were indeed beautiful sleeping angels. My love for them engulfed me, and I remember saying a silent blessing for the "wake-up call" of my life.

Terry got home every "night" by 3:00 AM, which made him available to look after the kids' morning routines and get them off to school. Then he would crash back in bed as my support staff trickled in throughout the day. Some days I didn't have the energy for physiotherapy, I just wanted to sleep and to not feel the intense pain that had been with me twenty-four/seven since March twenty-sixth. It just never went away. If anything, it got worse not better. But my home rehab crew always had cheerful smiles, motivating me to keep trying, no matter that my brain and body were yelling *No!* Recovery was not a smooth path forwards, and it often felt like an emotional battleground of two steps forwards and three steps backwards.

By late afternoons, I was back in my bed for good, as I had no muscle strength to do anything but lie flat on my back. I had already forgotten the activities of the day, because short-term memory issues continued to plague me. Terry would be waking up and getting ready for the kids to come home. He prepared the meals and looked after their needs until he left for work. His own exhaustion must have been tremendous. But not once did he ever complain to me. Although, at times, I wished he would open up to me about how this had affected him, his thoughts and feelings were elusive to me. But I knew he had a sounding board in others to relieve his stress and anger. His love, his support, and his compassion gave me strength to continue my recovery and not give up. When the children came home from school, they liked to take over and pretend they were my nurses caring for me. It helped give Terry some space and free time to get dinner organized before he left for work.

On Saturday mornings, they were all busy once more with a flurry of activity in the kitchen and bedroom. This was time for just the family. Before I knew it, I had a tray on my lap with a delicious breakfast made with lots of love: soggy toast and lukewarm, milky tea. It was the best breakfast I ever had and I loved every morsel.

I am very proud of the way my children have handled the whole ordeal. They have taught me so much, so resilient at times that I thought they were handling the difficulties better than Terry and I did. They have just adapted and given their love unconditionally. A valuable lesson we could all learn: loving without conditions; to them, love just is!

In Canada, many citizens have medical coverage, either paid for through their employers or individually paying for that coverage themselves. Here in Ontario it's called OHIP. Normally all medical tests are covered, and any bill from the hospital is nominal. You can imagine my shock and bewilderment when I opened a letter from the hospital with an invoice of almost three-thousand dollars. A *lovely* surprise. Unfortunately, we had no choice but to pay—I had agreed to it with a tortured scribble on confusing papers at the start of my admission. Apparently, I had been put into the first available bed, which just happened to be semiprivate (two beds). Terry's coverage was for *ward care*, which had four beds per room, even though no ward beds were available at the time. I felt that the system had failed me in every possible way. When the hospital staff had come around to have consent papers signed, they were fully aware I was suffering from mental confusion and was hardly able to comprehend the questions they posed to me. Nevertheless, they chose to proceed with the signing process without my husband present, at the time, I thought they were being helpful and felt thankful for their guidance. But I was in a childlike state, confused and frightened, and did what I was told to do with no comprehension of why I needed to do so. I had in fact inadvertently compounded my family's stress with that ridiculous bill from Joseph Brant Hospital.

When I received the invoice, I struggled through feelings of inadequacy that I had been unable to comprehend what those papers would mean to my family. Feelings of stupidity, guilt and anger were compounded by the fact that I did not receive medical or dental coverage from my employer any longer. A few months prior to the MS attack, I had switched my company's benefit plan to RRSPs, flex credits. The "Registered Retirement Savings Plan" was something new, and since

I had never submitted a dental or medical claim while employed, I thought why not? But my reasoning had failed me. I was left with a benefit package that provided "retirement credits", but not medical, dental, or other type of coverage like physiotherapy or massage, which would have helped in my healing tremendously. I had never thought any kind of disability could ever happen to me. Plus, I figured I'd try the transferring of flex credits to RRSPs for a year and if I didn't like it, I would switch back, as our plan had told us we could. I would pay a hefty price for that miscalculation.

No one knows what tomorrow will bring. No one! No matter what your employer offers you, always keep your medical. This invoice was a rude awakening to life with MS and the ramifications of that mental confusion that had engulfed me from March 26, 2006. It did teach me one thing: never to sign any documents until Terry had a chance to review them. It is worth the embarrassment of my own diminished mental capacity even if only one person reflects on this and protects themselves in case of full disability.

I had felt as though two distinct personalities battled within my mind. The woman I had been before the diagnosis came forwards, fighting for survival. The other part of me insisted I had to accept I was forever changed. As the months drifted by at home, it felt as though I were on a roller coaster. Some days I felt good and knew I was on the right path for healing. Other days it felt like I was never going to get better. That inner struggle continued to drain me. My emotions were neither easy to control nor to understand. The only way I got through was to take it one day at a time. If that seemed too much, then I took it one hour at a time, or one breath at a time. I thought PMS was bad! These emotional swings made PMS feel like a luxury cruise, while now, my very soul was a lost ship at sea, battered from all sides by hurricane storms engulfing its decks.

Previously I had tried to hide from other such storms throughout the recovery. Or I had fought them in battle, or resisted them by blocking their effects on me, even denied the existence of the emotions that surged forth in my recovery. It reminded me of my days learning to drive a standard transmission. I understood the concept of smooth transitions, but jagged jumps forward would be followed by a complete stall. I had to figure out how to let go of what I thought I knew and start again in the dark unknown.

For me it all boiled down to acknowledging my fear of that unknown, and that I was afraid. *I was afraid!* Once I fully accepted that, I felt my recovery move forwards a little more smoothly. Like the monsters in the closet as a child—once the closet was opened, the monsters seemed to have disappeared or certainly were reduced in size compared to what I had *imagined* them to be.

By the end of the summer of 2006, I made a conscious decision to let the bad days be as bad as they were, and that it was okay to have them. I am not sure if that happened because I was weakened by my inner struggles or if I finally figured out how to protect what energy I had. But it allowed me to accept myself as I was, in the *present moment.* I tried hard not to change the feelings, but to just allow and accept them as they were. That made them easier to bear, for I knew a bad day would eventually turn into a good day, continuing to deepen my understanding of "accepting what is". It took many repeated efforts to change the thoughts and behaviour patterns from my pre-MS life. To accept willingly those moments when I was lost within my fear and pain, within the unknown future. What had served me well before MS no longer served me. Even the decisions I had made then did not serve me now. So, instead of battling my thoughts and my fears as I used to, I welcomed them.

Fear can play tricks on your mind, and when your mind is already having neurological malfunction, it can be hell. Nonetheless, I dared to ask, *Why am I afraid, and what is it I fear?* My first thought was, *Holy crap, that's going to be a very long list!* Somehow though, it allowed me to look at fear differently, like a soul partner. I had conversations with it in my journal, writing about the grip it had on my reality. Trying to keep my sense of humor, these conversations often sounded something like this:

"Hello fear, I am rather busy right now, so please do what you must and move on".

And the fear would answer, "So, you finally acknowledge me and bring me to life. And now I control you".

And I would reply, "Thank you for visiting, but you cannot control what I have faced and released. There is nowhere you can hide within me, for you no longer scare me. Now get lost!"

I did the same with pain and with despair. Facing these things means acknowledging they exist, thanking them for visiting, and then releasing them.

Recovery was like a jigsaw puzzle, with me putting the funny-shaped pieces into place, half the time blind to the big picture. Fear was a large part of that picture, but the jigsaw pieces I connected were building my new awareness of life.

No matter how dark the cloudy days, the sun always shone brightly beneath them. It's like standing up to bullies—eventually they back down, once you have faced them and taken the wind from their sails. I sat in silence and welcomed whatever feelings or awareness came to me. I came to understand that each of these feelings gave me lessons that helped me gain strength within my spirit and soul. Like any student trying to learn something new, these lessons would take many repetitions before I truly assimilated the new knowledge.

Always somewhere in the back of my mind though—that left hemisphere would spontaneously come on line—"ramblings and what-ifs" continued pulling me into a vortex of darkness, despair, and sorrow. But on the right side, the daily awareness and acceptance of all the thoughts within me helped fuel my determination to live well, even with MS. An unsinkable, irrefutable inner guide of well being helped me move through these very difficult and painful times.

In the first year, a lot of information came my way about the disease, MS. What it had already damaged and what it could still do to me was explained fairly well by my doctors, nurses, and homecare support workers. Pam's big white binder continued to be a constant encyclopedia that provided knowledge whenever I needed it. On top of all that, I had Irma, my close friend and mentor who also walked her life's journey with progressive multiple sclerosis. I read and reread to learn as best I could, but with short-term memory issues, even that was a difficult challenge. If nothing else, I was persistent. Pam said I was stubborn.

But it was the actual day-to-day, and sometimes hour-by-hour, living and conversing with MS that helped me to understand and eventually move on. Doctors, family, and friends obviously helped, but unless they too walk their lives with MS, there was much lost in the translation between the facts and the feeling side of the disease. Truly looking within myself, was the key to my ability to live my life well with a neurological disease. Understanding the feelings within me—the emotions, the questions, the frustrations, the despair and, yes, even the anger, began to teach me the true depth of who I was. It took time, repetitive stillness, and patience to understand what my body, heart, and soul told me. It was a continuous search deep within for the direction of this new life I lived.

Again, I started to use easy meditation and visualization techniques to help me gain strength and find peace within the rambling thoughts that confused me. The more I practiced, the more I was able to step outside all the questions and find my own peacefulness, my own Divine stillness. It took patience, dedication, and determination to *repeatedly* quiet my mind. In essence, what I tried to do was look at my new life as if I were taking a new course, or creating a new formulation or, again, learning to drive manual transmission. Each day brought lessons for me to learn, and as I looked deeper within myself, I treated my recovery as a new opportunity to learn and grow. I may have fallen down repeatedly, either physically or mentally, but I always got back up and tackled the lesson again! I guess I *was* stubborn!

It was not easy to let go of my chattering subconscious thoughts. They were made up of everything from the past and everything that could be in the future, rambling questions, confused thoughts that seemed not to want me to *still* my mind. All of that is quite normal in the healing process, but I remember struggling with my need for peace to the point of meltdown.

One particular day sticks out. My head was in a cloudy or foggy state that matched the weather outside. I tried to meditate without much success. My frustration with myself mounted until I actually screamed at the top of my lungs—aloud or in my mind, I'm not sure—*Holy crap, will you all just shut up?!* But those noisy thoughts never listened to me; instead, the insistent chattering started up again and it seemed to have no end in sight. Then I realized they were all I had ever known—my mind was running on autopilot, its switch permanently stuck on! No off-button anywhere! The awareness of that craziness shocked me.

Decades before, I'd had tests on my brain and was told one of the reasons I had severe migraines was that it did not go into the deep sleep pattern called *rapid eye movement* (REM) enough; I seemed to function well on little sleep. As a light sleeper, I was always aware of everything around me even when asleep. I heard the cat walking through the hallway, the furnace going on and off, cars going by on our street, if the kids got up and came down the stairs. I could tell when my husband drove his car up our driveway after 2:00 AM and when he turned his key in the lock. I was asleep, yet I was aware of all the external sounds around me. My brain was overly active in a barrage of thoughts that kept me in an aggressive stance of self-completion—my goal: attaining some form of perfection for my self worth. The only time I was aware of self-control over my rambling thoughts was when I actively trained in martial arts. And that control was fleeting. It is rather a paradox that the devastation of multiple sclerosis would finally help me find the off-button for all this brain chatter.

The task of learning to quiet my mind was very similar to learning to walk again and to using my right arm. I had to retrain myself, retrain my brain. I figured out that if I could retrain (or remap around the damage) my mind's control of my arm and leg to do a function at my request, then I should also be able to train my mind to still my thoughts at my request. It was that same determination and repetitive practice that guided me to develop the *skill* of stillness and, ultimately, a sense of well being, without having to prove my self worth to anyone, including me.

In time, meditation and visualization would become the off-button. It took practice, practice, practice and more practice. I would repeat the mantra in my mind: *My own pursuit of inner peace and balance within is but one thought away,* until, more than just pretty words, I deeply believed them. Then I would sit perfectly still and let the constant barrage of chattering in my left hemisphere start to fade away. I steadied my breathing: inhaling deeply and exhaling slowly and calmly. On the inhales, I would imagine I was bringing into my body Divine healing energy. It's a bright, white light, only it doesn't hurt my head! And then, I imagined a new feeling of strength filling my body and mind. I pulled strength from a source that I variously called the Beloved, the Divine, and God. Soon enough, everything I feared released on the exhales.

These moments when I felt my soul expanding within me like a balloon began always in the deepest darkness. Their transformation was truly magical. Some kind of expansive knowledge already resident in my brain's right hemisphere would burst through the confines of ordinary brain function and I experienced happiness, peace, and love way beyond anything I had ever known in my life. It surged through me as strength; it gave me an extraordinary awareness of my spirit; and I glimpsed my authentic self. The challenges I faced faded; what I looked like, who I was, and even what I could physically do with this disease no longer mattered. What mattered was the energy within me—the energy within us all—that I could feel resonating deeply in my being.

These moments are difficult to describe. It was as if a warm spiritual light beamed into the parts of me where my despair resided. I was filled with a sense of inner purpose, a deep, all-consuming passion, and I needed to write. I would write day or night, journaling my progress through a disease that was becoming an awakening and, more importantly, into and through the *awareness* of that awakening. Finally, I was becoming the director of the movie called *My Life*. I was aware of the roles that were cast in the movie, the choices as they played out, and I was also aware of the movie as a whole, over and above the individual scenes. Whereas before this inner awareness, I had only been caught up in the scenes—first we do this, then we do that, then this happens, then that—the plot lines, and I'd thought *those were* the whole movie.

When those great energy surges came from within me, and those moments of peace, I rejoiced at *all life being as One*. Thus, I practiced stillness, silence, and reflection as much as I could, and it helped to guide me. The seeds of transformation were now forever planted and would grow into a power of well-being within me. This power had always been there; I was just unaware of its existence and unable to *consistently* tap into it until I started my recovery through MS.

We each have that inner power, that ability to step outside the limitations of everyday life and sense the universal spirit, God's energy mingled with our own. We can tap into that power because we are all part of it; we are all connected as One formless vibration of energy. If you are willing to stand still in the fear of "unknowing" and ask *who am I, and what is my purpose, and* then, with patience and faith, wait for the answers to come from within your own inner spirit, your soul will respond as mine did. At the right moment, as your external awareness subsides, you awaken to your power, the spirit within you.

It took some time for me to acknowledge and accept that awareness within me. My life was so different from what it had been that, at first, I didn't even recognize myself. But, as with any change in our lives, it just took some time to assimilate the new environment I found myself in and to become familiar with these new feelings emerging from deep within me. Feelings I could only describe as *spiritual,* even peaceful, a loving unity of oneness with everything around me. It was an internal energy that seemed to give me strength and purpose when I physically had none. Even as I searched within myself for an understanding of this new thing, I connected more deeply with it.

Everything around me seemed more alive and more beautiful, whether it was the birds, the trees, the sky up above, or the people walking along in life seemingly oblivious to the beauty and magic around them. I could feel a deep understanding of my connection to God, to that universal source that we are all a part of. When those deep feelings surfaced, I was aware of something within me far greater than I had ever imagined or even thought possible. My spiritual awareness guided me in those moments. Interestingly, my neurological pain also subsided to a tolerable level as fear was replaced with faith in the energy that I called my spiritual power within.

Three internal reflections became paramount in guiding me through the dark times journeying through multiple sclerosis: *Faith* that my destiny was unfolding as it was meant to and that I was fine, no matter the challenges I faced. *Loving* myself as I was, as I am, and as I will be. And then *accepting* how things were. I learned nothing was impossible when you accept *All* with faith and love. Your greatest tool is your authentic self, your inner power. Believing in that awakens the giant within. All the challenges I faced were but lessons, and I grabbed onto many things to get me past the waves of fear and discomfort, and through the great unknown of my life.

During that first year of diagnosis, I changed from a food scientist to a scientist exploring the journey of my soul, experiencing my own transformations within. I became able to sense my own recovery spiritually, as I released the old demands I had placed upon myself. Make no mistake, I was not fooling myself. I knew there would be struggles ahead. But the faith I grabbed onto enabled me to see the positive, to feel the positive, and to be positive as I recreated my life, the life I was now living with MS.

A thought came to me that only through the disease and loss could I fully awaken to my spirit, my soul. I wondered if a caterpillar, wrapped up in its cocoon, fought its own demise prior to bursting open and becoming a beautiful butterfly. How does the caterpillar face knowing it will never be a caterpillar again, but instead will become something it has never conceived of, never thought of in its previous lifetime? What we know is that a caterpillar faces whatever fear of change it has; it surrenders to the unknown and, in doing so, becomes a newly formed beautiful butterfly. Part of that caterpillar dies and part goes on, but it has faith in the Divine journey—whether it has awareness of that faith or not—and with that faith, continues its metamorphosis into its new form, the butterfly. We are no different. We're like caterpillars going about our lives as if that life is all we are. Will we become butterflies without any decision on our parts as caterpillars do? Only if we let go of the fear of our metamorphosis and let it happen. Becoming consciously aware of the greater universal source and accepting that we are much more than the life we have lived, allows us to become the beautiful butterfly with faith and love. That's when the most wondrous spiritual journey of transformation begins. That's what happened to me.

My belief in this power greater than myself gave me faith that a new purpose was unfolding in my life. Though I knew not what that purpose was. Sure, at times my brain continued its incessant ramblings bringing fear, anxiety, and depression. The more I subconsciously tried to fight these thoughts, the harder they hit me. It seemed to me the garbage in my head was capable of breaking my spirit, my very soul. But two words kept coming to mind. They did not seem to come from me; they were more like an echo. Sometimes I thought I was truly losing my mind, but the echo persisted, "Let go, let go, let go".

Somewhere deep inside I knew what I needed to do. The masks and defenses I had put up throughout my life to stop the pain and suffering had served me well. But it had always been the greatest depths of that suffering that had allowed my strengths to come forwards. And so it was now as my greatest strengths surfaced from my soul. Those old ways were suffocating me, and I was too tired to fight. As that realization hit, the walls hiding past and present pains started to crumble for good. I tried to face, acknowledge, and even accept all the challenges and lessons within my life. I faced the fear, the pain, and the unknown. In facing them, I released everything and truly and *completely let go.* Growing in its place was love, compassion, and forgiveness. This was not a thought; it was a feeling that started to surge forth from my core. Alas, I was not as instinctive as a caterpillar, so my transformation continued two steps forwards and sometimes three steps back. But the direction was set into motion, and I felt guided towards the calling of my destiny.

Of course, I was still operating on a day-to-day basis. It took ongoing commitment to stay positive and, when that failed me, I turned to nature and the beauty around me. That might sound silly, but it was in those moments when I had to exhort myself to not give up that nature came forwards to guide me. Sometimes I would suddenly notice the birds at the feeders outside my windows, or the way the branches of my two-hundred-year-old oaks swayed to and fro in a storm. I saw nature's beauty and somehow that eased my pain.

Use whatever you can to help you heal. Nature had a strong healing power for me. I enjoyed the garden from my window and frequently felt love and happiness returning to my heart. I was mesmerized by the chipmunks that filled their cheeks with my birdseed, only to run off and come back to tackle the birder feeder once more, as if they knew of a great, looming drought that would end their food supply. How big their cheeks do grow! I found myself laughing at all the little critters that seemed completely unaware that a strange woman was watching them moment to moment. Squirrels chasing each other at play, the hawk that perched upon my arbor as if it were king! I remember asking myself, *why did I not know I had so much beauty around me?* But I felt in my heart I had known. I had just been too busy to stop and give thanks for that beauty. I took the trees, the flowers, even all the animals in my garden for granted. I questioned whether I had taken my family, friends, and colleagues for granted. Hadn't I missed what life was truly about?

Soon enough, I came to realize that I had taken myself for granted too. My own mind and body. Remembering what I had felt about the ingratitude of some patients towards hospital staff, I realized I too owed more thanks than I had thought. I was determined to offer more gratitude, more freely, and more openly. I gave thanks for my window, my portal to the outside world as I sat in my wheelchair. I gave thanks for the garden that I looked out my window upon. And I started expressing gratitude for the blessings inside me too. At first that seemed hard to do. A small part of me was still yelling about all the negatives of a disease that had robbed me of my life, my career, and my ability to look after my loved ones and myself. So I would force myself to think of at least two things to be grateful for. It was slow at first, partly due to my brain difficulty and partly due to the fact I had never thanked myself or the birds before. Have you? Maybe it's time for you to take a step back from your busy life and look at the beauty of life surrounding you! As I continued with my thanks and gratitude, I felt more and more joyful—even peaceful—enjoying the simplicities in life that filled me.

Then there was the ongoing physical recovery. Rehabilitation continued to be a painful retraining, but with my husband, my children and my friends supporting me, I was able to reclaim parts of my physical self. My children helped me move my right leg when I could not get it to move. By the summer of 2007, I was able to walk a little—supervised—with my walker. Though I had days when my legs refused to do what I was telling them to, I was beginning to show consistent improvement. The light at the end of the tunnel was in sight. As the summer months passed, it became apparent that my left leg was also suffering muscle loss due to my inability to walk normally. I expanded the physiotherapy exercises to include both legs to help regain some muscle mass and strength in my left leg, which was still learning to become dominant.

My homecare workers made sure I was doing things safely as I would try to transport myself to the washroom, make small meals, or hold a cup without dropping the contents all over me. With the brain damage, I was apt to try things that were completely insane. Like taking the small casserole out of the oven without using oven mitts. Putting the wrong burner on for the stove and melting my carafe to a plastic puddle. Even having a meal in the oven and completely forgetting about it until the house filled up with smoke and the meal burnt to a crisp. I got sidetracked on easy tasks. Flooding the kitchen because I forgot I had put the tap on and then not turning it off. At times, I would not even remember what I was in the process of doing!

But it was important to me to reclaim my ability to contribute to my family. So my occupational therapist led my family and me to set up guidelines so that I could take on responsibilities while maintaining safety. My husband and children had to learn to recognize my limitations for those times when my brain failed me and I would inadvertently put myself—or anyone else—in danger without realizing it. In performing little tasks in the kitchen or getting around by myself on the main floor, I could feel I was helping my family as they were helping me. With their support and the physiotherapist's retraining exercises, I slowly started taking control of the physical part of my recovery along with the emotional and spiritual parts. As I did that, I felt the physical and the mental aspects of myself finally starting to come together again, to stay as one.

Pam and Irma continued to help me to see through the confusion and challenges that MS caused. They were strong enough within themselves to visit with me, sit with me, and not feel uncomfortable with the person I had become.

Irma had helped fuel my awakening, pointing out the infinite possibilities opening up to me. I remember thinking, *When the student is ready, the teacher will appear.* That was how I viewed myself, as a student learning from her vast spiritual wisdom. Her coaching was a great gift, and her friendship was food to a starving soul. She helped to point me in the right direction to inner healing and was at my side like a beacon of light. I am a better person because of her compassion and love. She understood me, she believed in me, and she honoured me with her spiritual light. I was truly blessed to have her in my life when I needed her the most. I love her with all that I am. Irma was an amazing mentor and friend. She became part of me; she became part of my family.

Pam and I have a deep friendship, one where words are not always needed. We were always able to instinctively know what the other needed. We did not always have to fill our time together with meaningless chatter or endless doing, but rather preferred sharing our innermost thoughts and reflections. Our spiritual connection was one of just knowing that no matter what, she would always be there for me as I would be there for her. The knowledge that I could release whatever was flowing through me. That she would be there not to change me, or judge me, but just to love and support me through the journey, to be with me while the pain swirled around my heart. That was Pam's true gift to me and it also fed my needs for positive support. We both understood how silence could be more powerful than any words used. We had shared happiness as well as sorrow. In short, we believed in each other, in our commitment to our friendship, as well as each other's growth. No disease or despair could ever take that type of commitment away. Both of my friends gave me strength and hope to look past any difficulties I had during my recovering.

Unfortunately, I lost friends too. Some were not able to come see me at the hospital. It takes great courage and compassion to sit with someone who no longer fits into the mould of "normal". I was no longer the woman, mentally or physically, that they had known. That kind of change can scare people. It is hard to sit and allow someone to just feel pain. Most want to change it, remove it, or can't even be near it, because it is too uncomfortable and unnerving. Those friends would transition and move on. I remember feeling sorrowful about it, even while understanding that I needed to release them and move on too. There were others to stand beside me, loving me no matter what I had become with MS. Either way, I became thankful for the old relationships that fell away as well. That helped me to release them. Everything that occurs in our lives is a lesson that helps our growth. Every person who walks through your life contributes to who we will become. I needed to learn and accept that lesson before moving on.

My journey through MS was largely a solitary journey, as it is for everyone, but it was comforting to know friends were there to catch me when I fell. They were a bridge between me and the outside world.

Getting around was so tirelessly difficult, the friends who stayed with me were always ready to help in any way they could. I am truly blessed for their presence in my life. They made such a difference in my healing and indeed my family's healing.

For a simplified list of the things I learned to keep in mind, turn the page.

Healing Steps to Keep in the Forefront of Your Mind

- Look to those who will nourish your soul as you heal. You will need their strength.
- Connect with people you can learn from, including someone who is already living well with MS. They will understand you and provide guidance when you need it.
- Find ways to laugh and celebrate life in the present moment. Remove the past *and* the future from your worries and concentrate only on the present moment.
- Be patient with yourself. Understand that any potential recovery and healing can at times be two steps forward and three steps back. This is a natural progression whether in self-healing or in making subsequent changes within your life and journey.
- Be your own courageous supporter, for only you can see the sunshine that hides behind your storm's clouds.
- Believe in yourself, love yourself, and be true to yourself.
- Stay away from those who may unknowingly shadow you with more negativity and sorrow. Those attitudes will compound your pain and lead you away from healing.
- If you are having a hard time deciding which is which, ask yourself a few simple questions and let your heart and soul guide you:
    - Am I more emotionally drained after spending time with that person?
    - Does it feel like "the life has been sucked out of me?"
    - Does your sadness increase; are you more depressed, do you cry more, after their visit?
    - Do you feel a renewed hope, some happiness after spending time with that person?
    - Do you find yourself smiling for no apparent reason?
    - Do you feel or sense light within you; do you have *more* energy?

Identifying what I needed to aid my progress was a pivotal moment for me. I bit the bullet and chose to put my own needs first. It was one of the very few times in my life that I had the courage and determination to follow my needs. Previously, my needs were the last ones I looked after, if I ever got to them at all. But with that monumental shift, I put a stake in the ground in front of me and made decisions about what was helping my healing and what was not. I worked on myself and asked everyone around me to respect and understand my wishes.

Some did not understand what I was trying to do by eliminating the negative pull, the hectic dramas of life, the constant chatter in our minds and in our conversations of nothing worthwhile, the complaining and ranting … these drained me physically and mentally. It seemed so obvious to me; I could not comprehend why it did not seem so to others. Family, friends, nurses, therapists, neighbours—the negative mindset isn't localized to one type of individual. I even noticed my husband and children succumbing to it unconsciously. But I was becoming *consciously aware* when it happened in me, and I was determined to redirect that energy into positive understanding and compassion. To be *aware* of my own negative thoughts meant I could take charge and release them. Others seemed unaware of it happening to them, as if they were going down on autopilot. I became a lot more conscious of what thoughts and conversations I would allow. Any repetitive negativity that was not a form of release, but rather a reliving and refueling of negative feelings, I attempted to stop. It was not a final end to them, however; they would reappear. But it was the *awareness* of them within myself that was important, and how damaging they were to the healing I sought.

Since I knew I craved peace, stillness, and silence, as well as time alone with myself where I could yield to my soul's requests for balance and well being, I started building a new environment to thrive in. I began to feed myself with what I would later call the "food that healed my soul": Inspirational books, CDs, and audio programs that helped guide me in my healing; music that soothed my whole body; my own writing; and being close to nature. These became powerful tools for me in my determination to heal my body-mind-spirit, balance my life, live well, and give back to others.

◊   Please find "Foods That Healed my Soul" for this list of tools and resources in the Appendix at the back of this book. They will surely help you too.

This kind of time was so important to me that sometimes I even wished I could have gone on a silent retreat into the wilderness. I could visualize a simple log cabin, preferably by a lake, it seemed the perfect image of what I needed to heal my bruised and beaten heart and soul. Lacking that, I carved that kind of time into my home life and healed myself. Some thought I was selfish or didn't understand my logic. Some even thought I was completely insane. But I knew. Logic had nothing to do it. I placed my needs first then laid the groundwork for a life that is balanced in mind, body, and soul. Balance is the key. I had to find the balance between positive thinking and pain-management, peaceful stillness and honest confrontation, relief and release.

To be sure, I kept my children's and husband's needs in the forefront of my healing process. They were witnessing firsthand the challenges I faced, whether it was from my arm or leg having uncontrollable spasms, seeing me unconscious on the floor as my body convulsed and gave way to pain, or experiencing the trouble I had just talking with them. Each indignity I endured, so did they. I learned that in being honest about what we were going through, they were able to deal with the fear that gripped their own hearts. It gave us each the strength we needed to continue to enjoy life and the blessings around us. To not take life and all that it entails for granted. We shared our fear and sorrow as well as our love and laughter. I will never hear the end of the tale of Mum passing out from a severe pain spike into the mashed potatoes, pork chops, and gravy one fine dinnertime. Although we can look back on that one now and laugh like crazy, I am still very thankful that Terry was too shocked to even *think* of a camera!

As time moved on, it was pretty obvious I still could not do even a little of what I used to at home. I was getting better at releasing control and asking for help—what choice did I have? But we were butting heads over the standard of living that I had always kept. We came upon the idea of family meetings to figure out how to best share the workload. We agreed we had to learn to work as a team and continue to learn from each other about how to proceed. Although the meetings were always asked for by me, everyone had time to speak, and we discussed a variety of issues before delegating tasks. That seemed to work … until it came to implementing them, of course! In retrospect, I think I learned the most by releasing both my need to control and organize as well as my perfectionist tendencies of what to expect.

It took me awhile to realize what was important to me was not always important to my family. They really didn't care about the dust bunnies floating alongside them. No matter how many times I tried to make them see how frustrated I was, they barely even noticed the existence of the dust bunnies to begin with. It never ceased to amaze me that they did not see what I saw!

But it went beyond dust. It was about lifestyle. Of course, we were starting over from scratch. But we only found that out in jumps and starts. A prime example was the typical stampeding rush home from school. There was always a panic with the kids all crowding into the doorway at once. All rushing in, and dumping their shoes, backpacks, and sometimes coats on the floor leading into our kitchen. They would be tripping over each other as they headed to the beckoning snack drawer, TV, or computer—everyone looking for their "chill out" zone after a hard day at school.

I could feel my own emotions starting to surge within me— frustration, disappointment, and even anger. The same litany of questions would spoil my recovery plan for the day: *Why can't they put their stuff away? Why am I trying to maneuver my wheelchair around the kitchen to tackle coats, backpacks, school lunch bags, and shoes? Why, why, why? The shoe rack is right there for Pete's sakes!!*

That's how the family meetings came into being. We all worked to bring clarity and understanding to what was indeed acceptable and what was not. The family listened, they heard, they agreed, they left … and it never happened. So now, as I tackle the after-school chaos, I am repeating to myself, *Be with peace and think loving thoughts.* Okay, so it's a little bit harder than that. And yes, I have moments when I think *Holy Jupiter, I am living with animals!* In truth, their father is no better, more often than not falling into the same kind of disarray. Here's my rant: I truly do not understand the difficulty in putting things away where they belong *after* being used. I mean, that way, it takes less time to find them later on. *Why,* I wonder, *is that such a difficult concept?* This theme has surfaced in every family meeting we have had, and I am sure it will be in every future one we have.

But this is normal life, right? I still have to remember to take a step back, give myself a moment to resettle my priorities—down to the soul level—and remember how they actually come in yelling, "Hi Mum! How was your day"? They may even swallow me whole in hugs and kisses as they drop their backpacks on their way to the snack drawer. If I keep tabs on *myself* and remain patient with them, they usually do come back and put things away ... after I have reminded them of course!

When I connect with my soul, I realize in the grand scheme of things a few backpacks, shoes, and *stuff* are not really such a big deal. My children, too, are my teachers. When we can feel love within and lead with that love and compassion for our loved ones, everything changes. Of course, I love them, and they love me, and how lucky and truly blessed we are. But watch out for those shoes at the door!

My family continued to adjust as well as they could to the realization that Mum could no longer do everything she used to do. That realization brought us to yet a new beginning for our family. They have had to become leaders within themselves as routines changed and expectations along with them. But it has made them stronger in many ways. They took care of me as I took care of them—with love and compassion. They have picked me up of the floor when I have fallen, or passed out from high pain levels. They are conscious of the fact that my leg and arm won't always move without help. They have been my eyes and my mind when both have failed me and left me in a cloud of confusion or emptiness. Yes, they have adjusted well beyond what I ever thought I would need to ask of them. I am not only very blessed and grateful, I am also very proud.

Sharing His Wisdom

If the words that flow through me
Guide others to inner peace and inner love
Then I have accomplished much in this life

I am as the words are
Open to interpretation, to understanding
Yet as they flow I am thankful to Beloved
For the abilities that flow through my wrists
I acknowledge the talent I do not own
And I ask for guidance
On sharing the words
That flow from my heart, my soul
To yours

Inhale the words deeply
Feel them enrobe and soothe your soul
Allow God's love to shine within
Through the words I pour
Onto pages and pages, with love I begin
To share with you
All that I am
All that I can be
That is my Divine destiny

Maureen Philpott Napier
January 15, 2008

Chapter 8

In Reflection

The summer of 2007 was quickly coming to an end; the children were excited to get back to school and see all their friends. I was just as excited, for the school routines allowed me to have my own quiet time daily to complete and concentrate on my exercises and retraining, not only physically but also mentally. The last weekend before school started, Terry and the children went out on their ATVs, driving through muddy bogs no doubt. I always marveled at the sight of them upon their return—man, child, and machine all covered stem to stern with thick mud. With the biggest smiles on their faces, they would recount how many times they got stuck, or how deep the muddy water was. Their happiness shone from them like a bright beam of light. It was intoxicating to watch them and listen to their stories.

My husband belonged to a group of ATV (also known as Quads) owners that called themselves the Mazinaw Mudders, and they surely enjoyed not only the mud they encountered, but also the feeling of becoming one with their machines in the natural paradise Bon Echo provides. (We are fortunate to have what we affectionately call, "our little cottage" on Mazinaw Lake, Bon Echo which is the same lake that Bon Echo Provincial Park is on in Kingston, Ontario). I saw something in these friends of ours that I cherished: these were adults who had the ability to *truly let go*, to embrace their childlike wonderment of awe and just have fun, completely free of the parameters we adults tend to put around ourselves. I shook my head and smiled as I heard the roar of their engines going off into the distance.

As for myself on that particular sunny and warm day, I sat lazily on our dock, my feet dangling into the warm waters of Mazinaw Lake. I was getting my retreat. The water shimmered almost too brightly to gaze upon. The waves slowly crashed into our dock where our boat bobbed up and down as if musically in tune with the waves. The wind felt warm upon my face. I could hear the loons calling their mates off in the distance, and I contemplated my life, my destiny's unknown path. I reflected on the abundance and beauty in my life, how everything as far as I could see felt somehow connected to me, a part of my soul. I looked up to the sky and said right out loud, "Thank you", to the Universal source I called Beloved, Divine and God.

Then the miracle happened. I can give it no other name. From the middle of my chest, I felt as if my heart and soul exploded joy within me. It was a feeling of pure, loving energy, as if a surge of electricity charged me with a different awareness beyond the life I lived. You might call it a phenomenon of expansiveness. All I know is, I felt a deep encompassing love for everything, including myself, and an acceptance of myself *without* judgment. I became aware of my spirit—it was me, but it was more than me, too—my essence, if you will. I awakened to the deep understanding—it was a sensation really—of this truth: "We are all One; Love is the key".

Nothing about my disease had changed. I still had all the difficulties and a paralyzed side; I still had trouble feeding myself without dropping everything on my lap. I still could not get my brain and motor skills to align themselves so I did not sound like a complete drunken fool at times and, unfortunately, I still needed all that homecare to meet all my personal needs, including getting help to dress. My life was still in complete upheaval, yet something within me had drastically changed. As if the floodlights had been *permanently* flipped on within the semi-darkened room that had been my previous awareness of my spirit and soul. Now the expansive feeling flooded every part of me, and I felt free. In that one moment, I was flooded with contentment and joy, a feeling of being *whole* and of being blessed.

As my recovery had proceeded, I had sensed fleeting moments similar to this one, but at a more superficial level. As if I had previously listened to the music of my soul at a lower volume. But now, the volume skyrocketed, booming within me and around me. This felt like beautiful fireworks, exploding from deep within my soul, the kind of grand finale that rains a spectacular array of colours high above. Star bursts and sudden big booms that almost make your heart miss a beat. That was the strength of this awareness of my spirit, or soul, or whatever you want to call it, coming to me and from me as I sat there gazing across the lake.

I still didn't know where I was headed, or how my future would unfold. I certainly didn't know what my destiny was or what path I would now be walking. I would still need to ask who am I and what am I here to do? But now, I sensed a clarity I had somehow missed previously. My passion for life bloomed and overflowed like the roses upon my arbor. I wanted to jump up and run to the nearest person, embracing them with the fierceness of my love and my joy. I wanted to run in the fields with my arms raised to the skies and celebrate life. I wanted to share what was flowing from me with everyone and everything I could see. Of course, I couldn't do any of that, but I wondered if sharing this feeling would cause a ripple effect, so everyone could feel this bursting love of life, all life as One, as I was experiencing it at this moment.

I knew I would continue to use my wheelchair, my electric scooter, and my walker to help me get around and conserve energy. But still, deep within me, I knew those physical limitations were unimportant. I would enjoy my ability to achieve smaller accomplishments, and I would live my life well, no matter my disabilities. Since March 2006, I had been recreating my life, pulling myself through the uncertainties of retraining with painful physiotherapy as well as my mind and physiological patterns from the moment I was diagnosed. So, wouldn't my internal reflections grow and strengthen my soul as I moved through my recovery? It made sense that as I took time to heal my mind and body, I would also heal my connection to my soul. My lifestyle had not previously been conducive to allowing the essence of who I Am, my soul, to come forth powerfully within my life. It was hidden behind an inner door I had closed long ago. I could visualize that door within my mind, what I saw was *majestic*, solid dark wood carved with the secrets of all time, what I am, my path, my destiny, and the Divine power within, *the Cathedral of my soul* blasted open and made its last stand to complete the profound awareness within me.

Prior to my diagnosis, all too often I never opened that door. I was too busy, I didn't have time, I didn't really believe in my own self worth, I'll do it later, I'm too afraid of what's in there, all these excuses kept my soul's inner door firmly closed. But every once in a while it would seek its own passage and slowly open, tempting me, it's hinges rusted it screeched in protest, and that is when I would feel the warmth of Divine light pouring from behind that door. Then it would abruptly slam shut once again as I focused my attentions on everything external to myself. The dark side often called ego would continue to mock me as it had done so before, the fool that I was, there's nothing there, and it's not real. I would have to consciously, in stillness and silence, not only re-locate the door, but also freely and willingly open it. My mind, body and soul were forming new bonds, somehow I felt guided, the knowledge I sought, but could give no name to, was behind that door. Just as I was healing and reconnecting my brain pathways to my body, I realized I was also reconnecting pathways to that inner part of me I had lost long before MS came into my life. And because of that, I would patiently take moment to moment to go within myself, in the quiet hush within my meditations, and search the depths within me to find and strengthen the power of my own soul.

This expansiveness of love and acceptance of *myself* as I was, at that moment, was so powerful that I had tears streaming down my face, not in anguish but in complete joy. I was completely free from the confines the disease MS constructed, as well as from the confines of my structured and controlled pre-MS life. Everything that I had thought I needed to be, or needed to do, to be successful in my life, to be loved in my life, seemed distant and not important any longer.

Though the difficulties or challenges from the disease would continue to affect my body and my mind, I came to understand that it could not affect my spiritual essence, what I believe is my soul. This was a *permanent* awakening of the beauty within this soul, a realization that through awareness and understanding, I released the power of my soul. The old saying "mind, body, and soul" took on a different meaning to me. I knew the disease MS could not affect my soul, and I felt whole, whole of spirit. And I understood that my life *was* in fact on course. I was on the *right* path, the *right* journey for me. I was *living* my destiny. That realization gave me strength beyond the physical.

> A deep need pulses within me and guides my journey to serve, to feel connected and needed within this life I live. To live my life with passion and meaning not only for myself, but for All.
>
> ~Maureen Philpott Napier~
> 2007

I believed in every fiber of my being that I was here to help others who may also be suffering. To help them find their own powerful healing and spiritual awareness through their disease. Could I share my experiences and thus share my strength? Could I have the courage and determination to see it through, no matter my physical and mental challenges? Could I stand amongst those I did not know and offer not only friendship, compassion, and love, but also a deeper understanding of the difficulties they too faced from this disease? In my most weakened state, that would now be my life. Could I be that strong?

Somewhere*

Somewhere a journey begins
At the end of the worldly
Existence we know

Somewhere a path stretches over
The stars
As the rivers of memories flow

Somewhere a silence is heard
Far away,
And the brightness
Of the day fills the night

Somewhere the trials of life
Are resolved into peace
When a soul finds its way
To the Light

Maureen Philpott Napier
February 19, 2004

* Dedicated to Mary J. Hanlon of St. Boswells, Scotland. My granny, my children's Scotland granny: Thank you for being my hero in my life, our love eternally yours.

CHAPTER 9

Tears from My Soul

We all have moments in our lives when we reflect back and think why did I not see that coming? How could I have been so blind? Then the inevitable questions surface, *Could I have changed my fate now, if I had awakened and acted on the problems sooner? Why was the problem not detected sooner? Whose fault was it?* Sometimes when we reflect back, we can be blindsided by confusion, dismay, and remorse. *How could I have done that? How could I have been so stupid? Why did I not grasp the gravity of these issues sooner?*

I was also bewildered and angry that the medical community had not diagnosed me sooner. I remembered my third pregnancy, while carrying my son Alastair in 1999, was excruciatingly painful midway through term. I lost much of the use of my right leg then, which I later dragged around until his birth. It was blamed on sciatica. After a natural childbirth, I was paralyzed, on *both* sides from the waist down. After some electric shock treatments, the feeling started to come back very slowly over the month. Within six months I was back to normal, with the occasional twinge down my right leg. It too was blamed on sciatica, yet my symptoms today are identical. No further investigation was ever done, and I accepted the medical team's reasoning. They were the experts after all.

In the years leading up to my MS diagnosis, I now see other signs that something was wrong. But I was caught up in my family, my career, my life's obligations, and I kept going and did not notice or pay attention to the signs. I had wrongly assumed they were the result of my hectic lifestyle, both personal and professional. But nonetheless, I blamed myself. I thought I was a fairly intelligent woman, so how could I not have recognized the severity of those signs? Maybe I would be able to walk today; maybe I would be able to take care of my personal needs; maybe I would be able to do for my family everything I used to do … maybe, maybe, maybe. What if, what if, what if!

All this was a pointless obsession with the past. Anger did nothing but fuel my ego's criticism of decisions that I could not remake and cause me mental anguish. I had no choice but to make peace with what had happened and release it; otherwise, I could end up messing up the present moment. The past was already gone after all. What decisions and actions I had made were carried out with the best intentions and the best information I had at that time. They could not be changed, and neither would I want them changed; they had built the foundation that made me, in my present life, strong. Why would I want to change anything in my past, when everything had paved the way to this awakening, to who and what I was now, even what I had now? These questions eventually dissipated, because I had *permanently* let the past go. Living in the present moment allowed me to start clearing my mind, to have faith and to accept that everything happening to me was indeed what was meant to be in this lifetime … and in this moment.

That is not to say that reflecting over your history is not a good thing … to a point. It helps to gain some understanding of the decisions you made, even the ones you missed—or thought you messed up. It's a good thing to take a closer look at your life and the challenges you face within this disease. Without dwelling on the why's and wherefore's. Sometimes you have to step back to see the bigger picture. That's when clarity and healing can take place.

In the following sections, I delve into what I consider my two points of reckoning *prior to diagnosis*. First, the loss of my grandmother, Granny, in February of 2004 crippled me in a way I was not prepared for. Her loss pulled me into a staggeringly painful vortex, my heart and soul's love, loss, pain, and need defeated me. Without her, I was not whole and struggled day to day with her loss imprinted on my heart.

The month was February 2004. I received the unexpected but inevitable phone call from my mother that *her* mother, my Granny, was in the hospital. "She's eighty-five; things do not sound good".

Granny was one of the anchors in my life; we'd had a special bond that grew throughout my life. I knew without a shadow of a doubt that she loved me—and that her love had pulled me through difficult and often painful times. I loved her with all that I was, body and soul.

In that weekend's pain and anguish, I felt as though I was losing the part of my foundation that had made me strong. Unexpectedly she was ripped from me, and I would have to release her, though part of me fought hard to hold on to her. Maybe it is always this way when you lose someone that is so ingrained and loved within your life. It seemed a test to my soul, to love enough to let her go and to celebrate her life and her contributions to this lifetime.

Though suffering from yet another severe migraine, I tried to get through to her at the hospital in Scotland. I couldn't reach the hospital switchboard, only a crazy, automated loop that held me on the line in a no-man's land of artificial voices and soft music. I couldn't get to her in time. I knew deep in my heart that she would have understood, but I felt as if I had failed her. An awful emptiness loomed in my heart and soul. All I could repeat through my prayers and tears was, *No, please not yet.* I had wanted her to hear me say, "I love you", one last time, but it was not meant to be.

My children came to me and sat on my bed. My head was still exploding, yet together we prayed and cried for "Scotland Granny", as they affectionately called her. We reminisced about our times together. I felt blessed that my children had had the opportunity to wrap their arms around her. Run and play in her courtyard. Giggle with her on the phone. Or, as they do still to this day, point high in our skies when they saw a "Scotland Granny" plane, one big enough to fly them "over the pond", as we liked to call the Atlantic Ocean.

My children and I had flown overseas numerous times since they were babies, and they have had the luxury of growing up and being part of their great grandparents' lives. As a family, we went as often as we could. Terry and our children were able to see for themselves nature's beauty in the Scotland, the land of my birth, that I cherished. How many children get to have such sweet memories of their great-grandparents?

We were blessed, having enjoyed time with them both in Scotland and in Canada. Early on in my marriage, their love blossomed to include Terry and then, ten years later, our children. It had warmed my heart to know they had not only accepted Terry, but loved him as if he were their own. We had many great times with my grandparents, singing songs that got the whole family laughing uncontrollably. Granddad sang his song, "The Wrinkly Old Prune" that didn't want its wrinkles; we sang together "Oh, You Canny Shove Your Granny Off the Bus". The children laughed and clapped along in bliss. After my grandfather's passing in 1997, it was just Granny. My family's trips "home", our monthly telephone conversations, and our letter-writing continued, as did our awareness of the love we all shared. But I was greedy; I wanted more time with her! Ironically, Terry had been reminding me to call her a few months prior to her passing. He was unusually insistent, as if he subconsciously knew on some level that she neared the end. At the time, I was so busy with business travel, I kept putting it off saying, "Yes, I know. I will". But I never did; My guilt compounded my loss.

She was, in many ways, my hero. She represented hope, grace, strength, peace, love, compassion, and understanding. At times, she was the beacon I looked to when my childhood was filled with the turmoil and pain that I kept hidden. She was going to leave me without a final touch. Without another "I love you", without a final good-bye. It is one of the greatest regrets in my life.

Everyone should have the chance to experience, with their own hero, the kind of love and devotion I had with my grandmother. Grandparents are outside the realm of the rules parents must dish out to instill values in their children. They can become a home away from home, a lifeline of love and empathy, a repository of fascinating stories of the wonders of their lifetimes and the world we live in. Who is your hero? Have you told them how much they have meant to you and your well-being?

Granny's loss *crippled* me in a way I never imagined possible. It pulled me into an emotional whirlwind for which I was not prepared. With much juggling, I booked a flight to Scotland in time to attend the visitation and funeral. I held myself together—that's what we're supposed to do, right? I was good at putting on a façade of "all is well".

But in reality, I felt defeated and cheated. In the emptiness and regret, I hoped our spirits still soared together.

I wrote a poem for her named "Somewhere" the morning of her funeral. I was so distraught I forgot to read it after I gave my eulogy of her from a granddaughter's perspective. She was an amazing woman to me, her character, her smile, her warmth and love, even her indomitable spirit shined brightly. I found the poem almost a year and a half later scribbled on an envelope and still stuffed in the pocket of the black jacket I had worn. When one loses a loved one unexpectedly, feelings and emotions are raw and laid out for all to see, but the feeling in that poem was full of hope and transformation. The aftermath for me was in some small way the *unconscious beginning* of my own transformation.

My grief flowed in the silent words written and then released. Writing was a saving grace, and I would squeeze in time for it every night before I slept, no matter how late it was or how early I needed to get up. I just needed to write. Even now, the ache can be strong, especially on the anniversary of her passing. Nevertheless, I have, in some fashion, come to terms with the fact that death is only a natural part of our cycle of life we all live, while love is an eternal energy that never dies.

My second reckoning was the hint of an internal understanding of what my previous writings had been trying to communicate within me. After diagnosis, I suddenly became *consciously* aware of problems I had *subconsciously* written about from 2004-2006. *Now* I understood my heart and soul's confusion in the feelings and thoughts I had written down as poetry or short verse. *Now* I could see what a powerful transition period I had been *leading into*. Small changes had begun, but I had only an inkling of some undefined inner moment of self questioning and unexplained feelings of loss, grief, confusion, love, compassion, and a *flicker of the need to keep seeking*. An unconscious soul-searching had begun its journey. Wasn't I like that caterpillar, still wrapped up in its cocoon? A glorious transformation was very slowly taking place subconsciously.

Whispers from my soul became louder as my evolutionary journey continued to move forwards to the climatic explosion within my body of a disease known as MS. But did it matter that I had been *unaware* of this transient knowledge and understanding before multiple sclerosis had viciously attacked me on March 26, 2006? After much reflection, I felt it didn't matter; the progression of this unawareness was in the past. But this *present moment* of consciousness and awareness brought me clarity. At *this moment in time I was aware,* and that is how I moved forwards.

My writing was like a bouquet of flowers that varied in colour and vibrancy—inner reflections, inspirations, love of nature, and happiness. Sorrow and deep despair also filled the pages. But it all seemed to feed a part of my soul that I had previously been unaware of. Whatever I wrote seemed to free and energize me.

It is inevitable that during our lifetimes we will face many challenges and climb many hurdles. While they will tax our abilities and our devotion to inner growth, each has lessons. I ask myself the following questions when I need help getting past the uncertainty of the feelings that seemed to boil up from within me.

> - What can I learn from this experience, challenge, or feeling?
> - Have I learned this lesson already? Completely? Or will it reappear until I do?
> - What do I need to *do* to complete the lesson now?

Whether through deep sorrow or supreme happiness, our judgment can become clouded when we *become the emotion* we feel, and take it on as our total reality, or mistake it for our identity. Rather than releasing it back into the universal pool. We can become consumed, fearful, drained, and even angry, frustrated, or lost. We may feel as if we are completely alone. The deepest despair can hit us hard when we feel painful emotions surging through us; often getting reenacted throughout our lives with new challenges or pervasive thoughts replaying the same movie over and over again. The flip side, deep happiness, euphoria, and elation can swell our pride and inflate expectations, addicting us to the highs that happiness can bring, with all its promises and glories. It was the latter to which I was addicted too. The pendulum swings wildly from day to day, month to month, even year to year. We either ride the wave or we drown in it, sometimes we do both.

My life had been no different in that respect. Each challenge, whether happy or sorrowful, left its footprint on my heart, and through the culmination of successfully cleared hurdles, I became what I thought was "me".

I left home a few months after my eighteenth birthday and became the leader and sole provider of my successful future. I can look back now and clearly see as I entered my teens I already had this inner drive to find *success*. I defined that success by my own consumption of knowledge; it felt as if that was the fuel to life. Consequently, I thrived on "study" and would continue to pursue courses, technical advancements throughout my career leading up to March 26, 2006. Like a hungry wolf, I pursued knowledge to fill my own expansive intellect. The hunger was never satisfied. The paradox of my life now, with MS, has been the loss of that knowledge due to the brain damage to my left hemisphere. A rather humbling experience that challenges me daily as I try to regain even some small way to help my children with their homework. Even small tasks within the kitchen where I have miscalculated ratios of water to rice, understanding and following recipe directions to guide Ainsley as she makes a cake can become a panic-filled nightmare as I realize what capabilities I have lost.

As my life's journey unfolded and time passed by, my driven perfectionism was always in a flurry of activity. My need *to do* more and my need *to have* more, I would later understand, chained my soul. My internal programming encouraged a kind of hyper-consumerism, always seeking more and feeling like I never had enough, or I wasn't good enough. More prestige, more success, more material stuff, more money, more of everything outside of me—and with all of that, I most certainly did succeed! No amount of money or material possessions could give me the inner peace for which my soul had begun to search. It was externally unattainable. But that was a colossal lesson I would not truly awaken to until after my MS diagnosis and subsequent rebuilding of my life.

One And All

In the beauty of this moment
In the silence of my thoughts
There is within me, a great Divine power
Known as my authentic self
It is my inner light within the darkness
It is my inner strength, though consumed in weakness
It is the quiet acceptance of what is
The graceful understanding of one's self
As energy, not as form
In the essence of thoughtlessness
There is peace, there is stillness
It resonates within the energy I Am
Merging as One with Beloveds Divine source for All

I know together we are strong
For we have faith within the unknown
And hope within the uncertainty
We have love within the fear
Compassion within our tears
If we stand at the edge of this existence
That we may feel is our reality
We can sense thy own beauty of thy soul
There is an awareness of Beloved
A power within this form of body
It is life, it is death, and it is All
In the beauty of silence
In the strength of stillness
Know you are with the universal power of One and All
And what we thought of as our reality
Is not reality at all

Maureen Philpott Napier
February 20, 2009

CHAPTER 10

Destiny's Call

Sometimes destiny calls you to walk another pathway, a deep feeling propelling you forwards. If you are lucky, it is a smooth, heart-aching pull, a quiet whisper that helps you change direction to fulfill a destiny you didn't know you wanted, or needed. It might be a lingering flame that consciously builds slowly, allowing your mind, body, and soul to ponder new ideas of change and what ifs.

But for many of us—maybe even most of us—it is a sudden, violent awakening. Truth's brilliance can bring blinding fear and resistance to the change before your eyes. It can feel as drastic as night to day. You might be pulled into a vortex of conflicting emotions and physical pain. The feeling of being totally alone crushes you. The concept of failure becomes a heavy cloak that drags you down. All you can do is hold on as the crashing waves of change beat against your soul and carry your days onto unknown shores.

Destiny is a funny thing. How do we know if we are following the path that we often call our destiny? If I had been asked if I was following my destiny (before March 26, 2006), I would have confidently answered, Absolutely! But that confidence would have been based on my *external life's successes*. Everything, including my family, my possessions, investments and finances, as well as my career, my title, my objectives, goals, and accomplishments, all blended together to become the identity of what I thought was me. I'd thought the path that I had planned out as my life was my destiny. I knew no other way to live or work other than what I had built for myself through my own blend of inner control, hard work, determination, strength, and need for success.

I did what most of us do: live, learn, and grow from the often-dreaded "mistakes" I had made. I worked hard, built a strong foundation for my career, and felt my life, my destiny, was playing out like a well-orchestrated concerto. I had brief moments when I glimpsed a Divine peacefulness and excitement about this life, a connection to God, but I knew not where the feeling came from. It usually whispered to me while writing, but it was always sporadic; as quickly as it came, it would also go, leaving me unsure of what had happened, but wanting more. I continued to look outside of myself to find it because I was certain I was on course in my life, steering strongly through the currents this lifetime presented me. How could I have been so off-track? And so very, very wrong?

As I looked back over my life prior to the diagnosis, I was somewhat shocked to realize just how infinitely out of balance my lifestyle was; it hadn't truly sunk into my brain at the time. The definition of insanity flashed through my mind: doing the same thing repeatedly but expecting different results. My lifestyle had been geared for high speed, high pressure, thus becoming a high risk for my health and well being. I was a successful woman, but there was no balance. I had kept searching for peace and inner balance as if it was something I could attain and secure for myself, like a bright shiny new trophy. My next success! But I kept getting the same crazy results; overworked, overstressed, a complete breakdown nipping at my heels, I had kept running, kept doing and kept rushing. I hadn't figured that *change* needed to be done at my most basic level. I hadn't figured out that I needed *to stop, to look around me, and then to question why I felt so off-balance, with my control slipping by threads.* I had been either unwilling or unsure about *how to change* what I thought were my ideals for my life, my safety net. Even though I was still achieving successes which fueled my inner drive, professionally and personally I felt dazed. How had my actions in life stimulated this separation of body and soul? This disjointed imbalance kept me somewhat in survival mode. Maybe that's why it's called the "rat race"; it felt as though I was running in circles, endlessly trying to keep up. *Could* I have stopped and gotten off the wheel of life as I lived it at that time? I suspected that everything I was going through now was a necessary part of my journey to unlock and discover my whole self.

My life had been much like a jigsaw puzzle, some pieces were already in place from long ago. Even the scars that I had thought I had dealt with—and dispensed with—from growing up surfaced again from the chaos of disease. Like a memory card never fully wiped clean. They were part of the puzzle too. I was finding out that it was the culmination *of all the lessons and scars* that made me who I was. I could no more take them away from my existence than take away the air I needed to breathe.

Looking back now, I understand my perplexity, as I can clearly see the differences between conscious and unconscious living. But at the time, there was no separation, just a mass of conflicting battles going on in and amongst my mind, body, and soul that I was only barely aware of. In reflection, Destiny *was* calling me, but I never heard her calls. Destiny and awareness were buried within these words waiting to be written. And out of them, the nonstop quandaries, questions, contemplations, and insights, grew the possibility of inner peace. Prior to March 26, 2006, my life's journey had tossed me about through plenty of grief and pain, as well as love and happiness, but I had always resurfaced stronger, *my identity still intact.* Destiny and success for me was a road map I had planned, executed, and controlled. But can destiny be controlled?

My conscious mind was not as aware of the inner struggle as much as my subconscious mind was. Consciously, I was consumed in the survival of getting through my life, my goals, and commitments. Slowing down or stopping was not an option. I was consumed by the hectic pace of the lifestyle I led, but aren't we all? Women are more prone to putting their own needs at the bottom of the "to-do list" when they are raising a family, maintaining their home, and juggling a demanding career. That type of accelerated living has become the norm for society today. We have lost the awareness, strength, and ability to put our own internal well-being first, and to truly understand the need for simplicity and balance within our lives. Many of us are running out of control. In a constant state of wanting more—more of what, it doesn't matter, we just want more!

When subtle changes started affecting my health, it was far too easy to lay the blame on stress and my overall workload. I continually did too much, there never seemed to be enough time. Truth be told, I lived in a continual, controlled chaos at lightning speed. Since I was not the only one facing that type of chaos, it seemed a normal way to operate! And I not only survived, I kept up the pace, always seeking and pushing for the next success, no matter what it may be. Any conscious thoughts on getting my well-being on track were soundly and permanently put at the bottom of my list. (If they even made it to that list at all.)

However, changes in my destiny were already occurring beneath the silent words I wrote. Now looking back, I can see my life was indeed shifting. An inner force was building within me that was pulling me away from the life of a research scientist that had been mine for over twenty years. Some days I wondered how I could have written pages and pages of verse with so little effort. The writing had its own life, its own wisdom. I was not even aware such wisdom existed in me. My writing reflected the echoes of a soul desperately yearning to be set free, and trying to find balance. That little light in my spirit began to flicker; that seed within my soul began to grow. That silent quest brought me the realization that there was indeed more within me. A new understanding, if you will, of what I was missing in my life; and it wasn't something I could buy.

How does one prepare for a sudden, drastic shift in the perception of who they are? Had my destiny already been Divinely planned out, and if so why did I feel so much despair? Had my inability to balance my life led me down the path of illness? Had I inadvertently sacrificed my *being* to the ideals of society today? Prior to MS, I had believed in the strength and leadership that guided me. Where had I gone wrong? The days and weeks following March 26, 2006, brought me to my knees. I crashed and burned, just as a family psychologist in the summer of 2005 predicted I would. What had originally started out as treatment for a child needing help with stress issues at school, thus counseling, would quickly turn to the psychologist identifying my one-way trip to breakdown if I did not stop and slow down. Her words came back to haunt me. "If you don't slow down and stop, your body will, with or without you". I remember repeatedly telling her "I don't have time to slow down, there's too much on my plate, I can't take time off I am too busy".

Time itself knows no end
If the journey of your soul
has yet to begin

~ Maureen Philpott Napier ~
2005

Who was I now? What would my life be now? My destiny now seemed to be like a ball floating on the ocean, bobbing along unconcerned which undercurrents would affect my direction and the future before me. I floated inside the ball, part of me feeling terrified and trapped, but another part of me, my essence, if you wish, was just enjoying the ride.

The waves raged uncontrolled as the storm intensified, destroying everything in its path. But as the waves settled, a new awareness and growth took hold within me. Much like a hurricane's consuming destruction, the aftermath would leave its footprint, but new growth would always take hold. It was the same within my soul, and my destiny would reveal itself in time. I had no choice now, but to listen to my body, partially paralyzed and mentally depleted. Whether it was a result of the disease or the fact that I had not picked up on the health issues earlier and acted on them did not matter. I had been forced to stop and listen. I craved answers to questions yet unformed. The hunger within me that had originally surfaced from deep grief and loss continued to grow, fueling the awakening of the spirit within me. In time, I would awaken spiritually and stand facing the aftermath of a life I thought I had mastered. Naked to my soul, I would stand in the unknown and finally accept what was now my life. The essence of what I was had come barreling through my soul, showing me my spirit and the power within that joins us all. It was as if the vibration of our Divine God said, "So, you have finally stopped trying to hide". And the truth of that resonated to my very core.

We all seek, in some form or another, fulfillment, happiness, inner peace, and love in our lives. Being diagnosed with MS has forced me to reconcile with the identity I had made for myself, and also made me keenly aware that I still sought fulfillment, happiness, inner peace, and love. So, has anything really changed? Could I still achieve those, could I still receive them with a dysfunctional mind and body, with a disease that seemed to consume my life?

> One needs something to believe in, something which one can have whole-hearted enthusiasm. One needs to feel one's life has meaning, that one is needed in this world.
> ~Robert Burns~
> (1759–1796)

As I look back at what my life was prior to diagnosis, I honestly do not think I could have changed my views to the extent that I have now without having had that paralyzing MS attack on March 26, 2006. I have emerged stronger within a new balanced identity, one that incorporates the successes of the old me, but that allows a greater energy of self to come forwards and shine.

The jigsaw pieces of my medical history had finally fallen into place, explaining the reasons I had felt so much befuddlement in my mind and loss of feeling down my legs over what turns out to have been well over a decade prior to 2006. It was not surprising I had so many "little issues" popping up in my life. I now had the reasons behind the health issues that I had been dealing with for so long, and this gave me relief.

In each of us, there comes a time when, through the depths of our own despair we have to search deep within ourselves to find the strength to face our challenges, our fear, our sorrow, and our pain. This had been my time to find out who I really was, to become infinitely connected to everything around me. To accept and have faith that the internal shift and perception of my destiny was indeed on course. Within this journey through MS, my spirituality, compassion, and love gave me an inner strength beyond what I had ever had before. As the months and years moved on, I came to realize the true gift I had received: deep awareness of my true self, the essence of spirit. That which had destroyed me had also allowed a rebirth within me, and that not only helped me survive the challenges I faced, but it was the true gift within MS.

Through multiple sclerosis, I have become aware of my ability to heal and live well side by side with a neurological disease. My soul's light shone brightly, my heart's love gave unconditionally, and my new life, *living well with MS*, was born. We may travel down different roads in life but, in the end, we all come to the same crossroads: death of body, continuation of spirit. I recognize now that our true journey, our true destiny, is the awareness and acceptance of the all-encompassing power greater than us that fuels the consciousness of our spirits. That's the power within, the power of your soul! That, which is within us all, connects us all as One, the essence of inspiration and the vibrational energy of God's source. That is the magnificence of the Divine.

As I shifted from short-term disability to long-term disability in my second year with MS, I had to have faith in my continuing journey, in the path that lay before me. At times, everything seemed so difficult I was unsure if I had the inner strength to walk through the shifting emotions of sadness and bleakness the disease put me through. Somehow though, no matter how much emotional pain or sadness threatened to consume me, I was always able to straighten up and tell myself, "Everything will be okay. I am okay".

My career was somewhere off in the distance where I could no longer reach it. Sorrow seemed to swallow me whole at times as I tried to reconcile myself to my new life without the drive of a career to create my self-worth. Even in my own acceptance that I was no longer intellectually capable of continuing as a research and development scientist. Though it had been hard to accept, I had little contact with my colleagues. Understandably, their lives had kept up that hectic pace, while mine had stalled. Inevitably, I was left behind, no longer part of the team. Life had moved on for the company, my colleagues, and me. I had no more control over, or even a participation in, the life I had planned and executed as a research scientist. That part of who I was had ended. I had to relinquish my belief that I had to be in control of my life. As I sought a deeper awareness of the universal Divine source within me, control was one of the biggest speed bumps I faced. The universal energy flow, would guide me if I stepped away from my safety net of inner control.

Within my second, and leading into my third year with MS, I came to understand that I would still have moments of despair; chronic neurological pain was a constant reminder of the disease progressing through my body. Rehabilitation had continued into my second year until that too had slowly ended, as it was felt I had reached my maximum potential in my retraining. I continued to keep up the exercises and looked to inner healing through meditation and writing.

Astonishing the specialists, I was able to regain most of the basic movement in my right arm, though I still could not write well or get food to my mouth with it easily. It also tires quickly, which causes the numbness to escalate, but my left hand learned to compensate well. I am much better with a keyboard than handwriting with pen and paper. On my really good days, I can possibly write a few words, but mostly I even struggle to sign my name using my right hand. It looks like something my kids wrote when they were two or three. I continue to train my left hand to write, and there has been some improvement. The extreme burning sensations continued to plague my right foot and hand. Short-term memory loss was still affecting me, but the impaired vision with flashing spots was now only sporadic, rather than constant. I had been able to regain limited movement with my right leg, which meant I could walk a little around the house with the assistance of my walker. I still had difficulties with food, especially meat and complex carbohydrates, which were difficult and painful to digest. There were definite improvements within my speech and my thinking processes— on my good days. Periodically, the pain would be high, and I would be unable to get my thoughts out, my speech slurred as if I were intoxicated, which my husband thought was hilarious since I did not drink alcohol. My body had its own way of dealing with the intense neurological pain—as it spiked, I still quite often pass out. Usually the spasms in my right leg and arm pulled me back to consciousness.

Susan (Red Cross, PSW) continued with my homecare. Without her support five days a week, I would still have had a difficult time not only living well with MS, but just getting through the challenges I faced each day. She has looked after my homecare since I was released from the hospital and has learned to understand me even when I don't make sense. She has often filled in the blanks for visiting therapists who did not fully comprehend how MS had affected my thought processes, my mobility, or the fact that I would lose consciousness quite regularly with severe pain spikes.

From day to day, the unpredictability of the disease still challenged me emotionally and physically, yet I knew deep within me that having multiple sclerosis did not define my life. MS was not the complete *end* of my life, but the *rebirth* of life. I had struggled through the disease to find solutions and answers to questions I wasn't even sure where they came from. Yet within that struggle, I came to realize my own personal evolution needed that internal awakening to fully grasp the beauty of God's light, and for my own inner light to brighten. I learned a valuable lesson the hard way. To live and cherish every single moment for what it truly is: an undeniable blessing not to be taken for granted. Living the present moment to me meant not continually reliving the past, nor projecting my life into the future. I learned to accept and live in the present moment, for that's the only true moment we all have, no matter who you are or what you do. As I searched within myself to find the strength to endure the challenges MS presented, I started to feel some inner peace and balance through the spiritual seeds of self love, compassion, forgiveness, and my Divine faith.

The Beginning at the End

Cliffs lay staggered and worn
Through Mother Nature's glorious storms
She stood atop
Arms open wide
Accepted the power released by the sea at her side
As far below waves crashed ashore
In the mists of the sea
She could see eternity
Her heart and soul were
Jagged and torn
Like the cliffs she stood upon
But the beauty she saw
As the sun shone
Brought the strength she needed to go on

For what she thought was the end
Was actually the beginning
In the depths of one's heart
The seeds need released
For the journey of one's soul to be complete
She understood at that glorious time
That Beloved had stood by her side
Shared her pain, confusion and tears
Never left her alone to face her fears
So as her face was warmed by the sun
Her body cleansed by mists from the seas
Her soul soared and felt finally free
Beloved had given her His love and peace

Maureen Philpott Napier
January 24, 2007

CHAPTER 11

The Beginning at the End

I received my diagnosis of MS over three and a half years ago now. The process of recovery and healing has transformed me in mind, body, and soul, bringing me to a spiritual realization of who *I Am*. I came to understand that in my previous life, pursuing standard definitions of fulfillment, greatness, success, love, and perfection in my career, home, relationships, and even my possessions, I had lost some essential part of myself. Then, I lost myself totally in the despair of being diagnosed with a progressive, destructive disease that at present has no cure. I lost the spiritual guidance I had always taken for granted, forgotten my deeper knowing of the universal source that connected us all. The journey back to life, over the past three years, has been as challenging as it was rewarding. On days when I felt so weakened from the excessive pain and fatigue that I questioned how I could go on living, I continued to find somewhere deep within me, hope. This gave me strength to ride the wave until the pain subsided.

Everyone it seems needs, in some small way, praise, admiration and recognition, to be acknowledged that they have meaning and purpose in their lives. I want to help; I still want to serve. Too often though, it turns into a need to acquire things, to have anything and everything; but that search has no end. Our Western culture is at the peak of consumerism, the peak of excessive waste, and at the height of inner spiritual neglect. A deeply embedded ego continually fuels

Divine absence instead of *One* collective Divine presence. We are too externally focused, on too many goals, on money and possessions, on titles and success. I too lived that life. But to receive what's really valuable in this life—inner contentment, peace, even love—there has to be a balance. I most assuredly did not have that balance in my life prior to my diagnosis of MS.

Clearly, I was given a difficult challenge in this lifetime. I decided to take it as a lesson to help spur my awareness of the internal evolution my soul was yearning to seek. Even though, the path was often dark, painfully hard, and exceedingly lonely. At times, I too sank into the emptiness that multiple sclerosis can pull anyone into. Eventually, I ceased fighting against what I came to feel was a kind of *preparation* of my soul. A spiritual strength and beauty—that is within all of us— seemed to continue to awaken and strengthen within me as I journeyed through my recovery. I found that elusive inner balance—surely a blessing in disguise considering the challenges I faced daily with this disease! MS forced me to acknowledge the existing imbalance that kept me from the truer life force within me. God's light, His love, His acceptance, His forgiveness, seeped into me while traveling through my healing process. I had to sit there, captive, and face all my failures (as well as my successes) and all my weaknesses (as well as my strengths). I had to face my fears, release my control, and understand that I can't always meet the expectations to which I tried to hold myself.

As I continued on that healing journey, I finally became aware that I had truly accepted myself as *I Am for the first time in my life*. To do the best I could on this journey, to nurture my spiritual growth—the steps within this journey became more important than striving for perfection and excellence outside of myself. The paradox of knowing who I am now meant I walked through the maze of who I was before MS. I embarked on this journey that brought both dark and light, both strength and weakness, together as one whole. A revelation I suppose and transformation almost as astonishing as the caterpillar to butterfly.

I was now content in being no one in particular, except a woman searching to enlighten herself and enrich her soul from the inside so that she may serve others. I was content in the understanding that I needed to close doors to parts of my life that no longer fulfilled me. Content in not standing out in the crowd through excellence, successes, rewards, and possessions, but quietly knowing I had everything I needed to enrich my own life as well as those around me. I was content in exploring the vastness inside me that is connected to the Divine energy source of the universe. That source I variously called the Beloved, the Divine, Holy Spirit, and God. If you use a different name for the Divine energy that we are all a part of, I respect your choice, whatever it is. I believe the names humans use can never fully define the vibrational energy itself, but I know without a doubt we are *all One energy.* I need not understand how; I need not understand why; with faith I just know.

At one time, I was all action and no rest, no stillness. Like some wild, weird mixture of Super Hero and Energizer bunny, I completed tasks and duties with intense concentration, proving my value. Relentlessly performing and achieving the next gold star. Eventually, I completely drained my energy reserves and had nothing left within me, except an emptiness that consumed everything that I was. As I was hit with MS, I had absolutely nothing to give, even to myself. I was pulled into nothingness, deep, dark and foreboding nothingness—*I was nothing.* How can one find her way out of emptiness? It is interesting how our bodies and minds have given us the way to spirit in times of stress. It is through our own inner stillness, that the respite our soul needs to rejuvenate and bloom takes place. One of the many lessons I learned through having MS was the simple need to rest and rejuvenate my whole being—mind, body, and soul. Ignoring that need shut my body and mind down completely for days at a time. It was a hard lesson for me to learn. It was an enormous challenge for me to release old thought patterns and behaviours, so that I could lead a more balanced and fruitful life.

There's *something* within each of us that can pull us into a negative replay of old feelings, as if there's a surviving need for sorrow, pity, and the usual despair. The woeful lament of *Why me?* replaying over and over in our minds. It took me a long time to accept that I had some of that "something" in me. It was screaming about all the presumed injustices that I had lived through from childhood up to and including MS. The crisis of MS had certainly played out on an emotional battleground, in addition to the physical one, with the suffering replaying in my mind with a power all its own. Many great spiritual thinkers call that *something* the "ego" or "false self".

I must admit I had a hard time with that word. Ego was not something I wanted to think I had, much less *acted on* in my life. I believed I was a team player, a quiet but firm and conscientious leader, who gave of herself willingly to help others, to guide others for the benefit of the whole team, whether company or family. I was not out to serve the individuality of myself. I made mistakes, sure, just like everyone does, but surely they were just part of being human. But being sick forced me to face the moments where I threw adult tantrums and got caught up in anger, hate, negativity, and a compulsive need to be right or in control. I had to realize my ego or false self had been the part that kept replaying all the suffering. The list of wrongs against me would pop up whenever I was in a weakened state, which the disease placed me in frequently. *A great time to pounce and attack,* thought this sad part of me from its dark hiding place within.

It was the word *ego* that I did not like. I preferred to call it my "gremlin". But it really didn't matter what word put the description to the fact. What was important was my awareness that it was true. I felt it; I sensed it; and it had life within me. There were times when the replayed negativity crashed like stormy waves against my heart's shore.

But as I brought my own conscious awareness to these recurring thoughts and habitual actions, I was able to stay more firmly rooted in my authentic self. By consciously leading my attitude with positive affirmations and inspiration rather than negative thoughts of desperation, I was able to reduce the reruns of suffering. In turn, that diminished the ego's power.

There are very few among us who could claim to have lived their lives completely without ego, or that false self, popping up from time to time. Nevertheless, I felt ashamed that this part of me kept flaring up, maintaining the negativity and despair that seemed to follow my life. However, *becoming aware* of that gremlin was paramount. It allowed me the *awareness* of my pain and suffering, but stopped me from ballooning it out of proportion.

My gremlin thrived and survived by keeping me in a perpetual state of reliving my haunted past through the present pain and suffering of MS and the migraines exploding in my skull. It used anything and everything it could get its greedy little hands on, and it fought for its own survival within me, filling my head with self-hatred—in the reflection I saw, the life before me, and the past I had lived. My false self had dreamt of some future time when inner peace and freedom would be my life. But this reality only existed in the future. In *only* letting me dream of the future, that gremlin had tried to keep me away from living in the present moment. Yet I was realizing that the ego within was never satisfied and would always want more and more to fill it.

But it's my belief that when the ego surfaces, it also offers the opportunity to become consciously aware of it. That's what provides the deeper, meaningful lesson, a lesson that can help you ignite love, compassion, and forgiveness, especially when directed internally to your own heart and soul. When I looked deeply within myself, I was able to grasp that lesson and heal. Learning to love myself, to be good to myself, to nourish and heal myself from within awakened the spiritual beauty inside me that my false self had denied I even had.

The battle with ego can feel like being suffocated, but once you can see through it, the beauty of the soul emerges. Ego cannot live in the present moment. But as with anything, the commitment to live well, inspired from the depths within me would blossom and nourish my soul beyond ego. It was through the despair and pain that I would find the door to rebirth and be able to rejoice at the awakening of my soul. Having compassion for my suffering and loving *me* in the present moment removed the power of the negative ego. I felt like a stone thrown into the pond, rippling a new energy from all parts of me. The ripples sent my energy to everyone who surrounded me, but I never felt depleted. Rather, I was more energized. I had finally found the exit from the maze of self-negativity, and the proving of self worth. *Freedom was right here.* I created for myself a mantra that became a great measuring stick for where I was in the healing process of my mind: **Awareness, Acceptance, Release, Growth,** and then **Healing.** *(AARGH!)*

Celebrating the magnificence and beauty of all universal life *as One* continually grows within me. Maintaining my sense of peace, being patient with myself, and accepting the lessons as they unfold help me on this soulful journey. As with any journey, there were (and will be) twists and turns; steep, rugged inclines; even cliffs with slippery, sudden drops to the unknown. But now I know those are just other parts of me.

Today, I am able to tap into the power within my soul, to feed it, nurture it, and watch it grow within me. I can also sense the negativity when it rises in me. I take a moment to bring conscious thought to it and become aware of the impact that thought was having on me: muscles tensing, anger building, the negative chattering in the brain that rambles on its own accord. As I shift my awareness away from the ego's negative destructiveness and remember there is no right or wrong, only lessons and growth, it takes the power away from the ego side of pain, failure, the addiction to "being someone", or collecting more possessions.

What has transformed through healing and self-discovery has been my core beliefs about life, happiness, and contentment, about what is needed to be a success, a valued contributor to our world. While others may have thought that this neurological disease was the end of whom and what I had been, I chose to see it as a *new beginning*. Both views offer powerful lessons that can fuel personal growth and build strength to walk through life with a disease that continually challenges.

What I have since realized through writing, is that any time an emotion comes up, it can be written, read, acknowledged, and then released without judgment. Writing helps to remove me from the suffering of the emotion. What some spiritual traditions call *detachment*. If I don't judge the days in my life that have brought me the most happiness and contentment, why would I judge those days that have brought sadness and suffering? Both are just lessons on the same swinging pendulum called life. Even my limiting fears of being incomplete fade with this process.

The silent word has given me my sense of purpose throughout my journey with MS. Everything I sense around and within me pour through silent words. Besides enabling me to release the control any emotional thoughts have on me, writing nourishes my soul. I can now comfortably sit with great joy and happiness as well as with the darkness of deep sorrow. I can let the tears fall without the shame or discomfort of trying to hide them. Crying this way has also become part of healing. I may walk through my continuing journey stumbling and falling, yet with each step I keep Divine inspiration as my light. It guides me when I feel lost, it gives me warmth when the world feels cold and, in the end, it gives me back my appreciation of the beauty, awe, and wonderment of All life within this universe.

> Obtaining silence and stillness
> within my mind
> Is like finding the pot of gold
> at the end of the rainbow
>
> ~Maureen Philpott Napier~
> 2009

Look within yourself and see that you are already a success! You were perfection and success the day you were born into this life—without money, external identities, or a multitude of possessions. When you were born, you needed only love and nourishment; why must it be different now? We are all here to experience everything life can offer on our journey, but not at the cost of losing our authentic self, the power within us. Our soul's power is much like a compass, it offers guidance and then waits to see which path we will choose. Forever supportive, it guides us through our lessons, our pathways to personal growth; and then, upon completion, new lessons begin. The power we all seek is within us, not outside of us. When we truly realize this deeply within our soul's being, we can accomplish great things that have nothing to do with money, possessions, titles, or greed; but everything to do with inner peace, compassion, forgiveness, faith, hope and, most important of all, love. When we *All* awaken to that truth, there will be no hunger in the world, no war, no hate, because we will know we are all connected together as *One energy.* Therefore, what we do to others we also do to ourselves.

Realizing these simple truths was the beginning of life for me. And I am eternally grateful for all the blessings and lessons I've received on this journey. I continue to strive to live my life with inspiration and positive reflections, guided by awareness from my soul. I cherish the moments within life, not the minutes within life. The challenges I face with MS teach me to have patience for my own ongoing, healing journey. I cannot know what this progressive disease will do to my mind and body, but I do know it can never touch the essence of who I Am. I have learned from this ordeal that I need nothing outside of myself to realize great happiness, internal peace, and love. I have learned that balancing your spirit awakens the great spiritual power of your soul.

MS is part of my life. This I have accepted—no longer in turmoil, but with peace. In those moments that challenge me with pain, exhaustion, and the many other effects of MS, I surrender and accept with the words, *This is what is ... for this moment.* The great saying from wise King Solomon, "This too shall pass", is absolutely true; for better or worse, it always does. To be able to experience the greatest joys of success and happiness, we must also be able to experience the greatest depths of despair, sorrow, and pain. It's part of being whole, authentic. Each has value; each provides unique "learnings". No matter where you are on your journey with MS, your inner soul offers the key for inner healing and inner peace.

You must believe in the power within yourself, in your hidden strengths, and have faith that you will be all that you are meant to be. Use whatever means you have to live your life fully and passionately. Know from your soul that the little sparkle of light within is worth facing any fear that may surface, because once faced and accepted, they simply fall away. Once you have found stillness and silence within yourself, your internal power awakens and shines brightly from within you. Do not walk at night fearing that daylight will never come. Trust and believe in the universe; the light will come, it always does. It comes from the centre of the darkness that challenges our souls. Know as you walk in fear's darkness that having faith makes the darkness fall away, revealing your light, your inner power to *All.*

> Loving and accepting ourselves as we are
> is the greatest healing tool we have,
> for it allows inspiration to flow freely
> from the Divine,
> lighting up our souls like beacons to share
> our love with All.
>
> ~Maureen Philpott Napier~
> 2009

As you continue on your journey, you will have new dreams. They may seem smaller than your previous life goals. Or they may be much bigger. Mine are inspired from within and offer me more than I could have ever imagined. To live my life fully with continuing enthusiasm and passion means I live my life well, one moment at a time. I hear the Divine whispers as *One* voice, no matter what struggles I am wading through or how brightly the sun may shine on our family. To accept His grace, this awakening of soul, means it is with me always. In my strength as well as in my weakest moments, I thirst for a spiritual connection to my most inner *be-ing* of soul. I have a raging need to be One with the great mystery of the Divine, to release me from the suffering of this neurological disease. There is now compassion for All creation, a gift brought to me from the depths of my own solitude, silence, reflection, and in my own prayers of gratitude. I find myself repeatedly requesting patience and guidance as I learn and grow through my days.

Our family's new path, new balance, new beginning within the duties and responsibilities living this life bestows faith, love, understanding and compassion for each other upon us as we walk through this change. On days when my husband and I argue over what seems trivial to him and monumental to me, I often wonder how we will survive the aftershocks of change. His feelings and emotions are protected by his natural shield. I have no shield; I lay all that is within me in a quivering pile at his feet, wondering how else I can let him sense the true depths of my heart and soul. I want to share the awe of this journey's transformation within me, even through the disease, yet he is not at the same point of inner awareness as I am. I can sometimes see the glazed look in his eyes, and I had to finally stop trying to control his steps along his own journey. I was hopeful he would catch up to me, pompous fool that I was. It is not my journey; it is his.

Courtney, Ainsley, and Alastair are stretching their wings of choice and independence too. As I have journeyed though this disease my own determination to seek healing within my own *be-ing* has given them another way to look at life. Their list of "wants" has transformed into lists of "how to help", or how to serve others. I can love them, support them, and even guide them, but each has her and his own journey to walk. I hope that the foundation we built as parents has protected and nourished their hearts and souls. When the time comes, they can stand upon that foundation, test their wings and, with a final look over their shoulder, take flight and soar.

Having a progressive disease has never taken anything away from my feelings towards my family. In fact, it brought an acute awareness of gratitude for the awakening and blessings in my life. They are the roses along the path I walk; I drink in their beauty and wisdom; I am enriched with their love and tenderness. I think of the beauty of the rose, the vibrant blooms, and the sweet fragrance inhaled deeply … and then, along its stem are those sharp thorns that can dig deep into your skin. Life I believe is much like that. We mustn't complain about the thorns, when we have such fragrant blossoms to enjoy. The artistic creation of writing, the visualizations I have of dancing and twirling with my children amongst the summer's tall grasses, these feed my soul, allowing my love to continually bloom. It does not matter what disabilities or challenges I face. This journey was a quantum leap of the human heart and soul, of a family's love and commitment to each other. The most significant gifts in my life I took for granted—my family and friends, my health, love and laughter. This journey has been a passionate rebirth of who I am now.

My ultimate calling was to write this book, a journey in itself. As I release this energy out to our world, I sense a harmonizing union of spirit deep within me. I am less worried about the troubles external to me. My illuminated path is ever-unfolding through internal landscapes of grassy meadows, steep and rocky mountains, desolate deserts, and raging seas. Yet, I trust in the universal source pulsing through us all to guide *me*, and it does. The complexities of progressive MS will continue to challenge me on this life's journey. Yet I do not dwell on those difficult times, rather I prefer to see them as an opportunity to seek more rest, solitude, and inner reflection. Truth be told, I do not dwell on what my destiny holds, but rather choose to enjoy the rugged journey as it unfolds.

What I do believe from my very heart and soul is the passion and ability to express words that will bring faith, hope, wisdom, and (hopefully) healing to others, including you. I continue to hold onto faith, to seek inspiration from everyone and everything, and alignment with the vibrational energy source of Spirit. All of this means only that I am free to enjoy the beauty of All life. An all-encompassing love lights up my path as I mingle with the harmonizing union of Divine Spirit. And as it shines on me, so shall it shine on you.

APPENDIX

FOOD THAT HEALED MY SOUL

A Few of My Favourite Books:

Gregg Braden:
- *The Divine Matrix:* Santa Monica, CA: Hay House; 2007.
- *The Spontaneous Healing of Belief: Shattering the paradigm of false limits.* Santa Monica, CA: Hay House; 2008.
  www.greggbraden.com

Rhonda Byrne:
- *The Secret:* New York: Atria Books/Beyond Words Publishing; 2006, based on the DVD by TS Production LLC; 2006.
  www.thesecret.tv

Sonia Choquette:
- *The Answer Is Simple ... Love Yourself, Love Your Spirit:* Santa Monica, CA: Hay House; 2008.
  www.soniachoquette.com

Dr. Wayne Dyer
- *Being in Balance:* Santa Monica, CA: Hay House; 2006.
- *The Invisible force:* Santa Monica, CA: Hay House; 2007.
- *Change Your Thoughts, Change Your Life:* Santa Monica, CA: Hay House; 2007.
- *Your Ultimate Calling:* Santa Monica, CA: Hay House; 2008.
  www.drwaynedyer.com

Eckart Etolle:

- *A New Earth: Awakening to your life's purpose.* New York: Plume; 2006.
- *The Power of Now: A guide to spiritual enlightenment.* Novato, CA: New World Library and Vancouver, BC, Canada: Namaste Publishing Co.; 2004.
  www.eckarttolle.com

Louise L. Hay:

- *You Can Heal Your Life:* Santa Monica, CA: Hay House; 2007.
- *Heart Thoughts: A treasury of inner wisdom.* Santa Monica, CA: Hay House; 2005.
  www.louisehay.com

Denise Linn:

- *If I Can Forgive, So Can You:* Santa Monica, CA: Hay House; 2005.
- *Four Acts of Personal Power:* Santa Monica, CA: Hay House; 2007.
  www.deniselinn.com

Gladys Taylor McGarey, MD and Jess Stearn:

- *The Physician Within You: medicine for the millennium.* Deerfield Beach, FL: HCI Books; 1997.

CDs: Brain Remapping/Retraining:

Centerpointe Research Institute:
- *The Holosync Solution, Awakening Prologue:* Beaverton. OR: Centerpointe Research Institute; 2007.
  www.centerpointe.com

Dr. Jeffrey Thompson:
- *Alpha Relaxation System:* The Relaxation Company; 2000.
  www.therelaxationcompany.com

CDs: Positive Reinforcement and Healing:

Dr. Wayne Dyer:
- *Inspiration Your Ultimate Calling:* Santa Monica, CA: Hay House; 2006.
- *Secrets of Your Own Healing Power:* Santa Monica, CA: Hay House; 2000.
- *The Secrets of an Inspirational Life (In-Spirit):* Santa Monica, CA: Hay House; 2006.
- *The Essence of Being in Balance: Creating habits to match your desires.* Santa Monica, CA: Hay House; 2006.
  Wwwdrwaynedyer.com

Caroline Myss:
- *Entering the Castle: Exploring your Mystical experiences of God.* Santa Monica, CA: Hay House; 2007.
- *Finding Your Sacred Contract:* Santa Monica, CA: Hay House; 2003.
  www.myss.com

Mark Stanton Welch:
- *Attunement to Higher Vibrational Living:* Santa Monica, CA: Hay House; 2005.
  www.markstantonwelch.com

ACKNOWLEDGMENTS

My deepest love and appreciation to:

Courtney, Ainsley, and Alastair: My beloved children, you are the light of my world. I am forever blessed to have your unconditional love, understanding, and forgiveness (when I seem unfairly harsh). Your strength and wisdom have taught me much about myself and my journey. I love you with all that I am. Your positive support was the fuel that fed my soul and helped me to push forwards through the challenges I faced. Thank you for never giving up on me, for sharing not only your compassion, but also your strength. How proud I am to be your mother.

Terry: Can you believe twenty-five years have passed since we first met? I can't help but smile at the memories of that day. How I overheard your cocky comment to a friend, "She's the one I'm going to marry". I wanted to run in the opposite direction! I often wondered *how* did you know, *how* did you have such strong faith in something that had not yet been born? And more important, how did you have faith in me, when I had not faith in myself? Our friendship soon blossomed into love and marriage. Our journey together has had many highs as well as lows. Somehow, we were able to weather those storms and continued supporting the friendship we began so many years ago.

While we managed to navigate through the changes within our lives, our marriage seemed to mimic the seasons Mother Nature provides, maturing and growing stronger as the years passed. Therefore our life and love kept being reborn. This, I believe, is our greatest legacy to our children. We have faced our storms, enjoyed the winds of change, and felt the sun's everlasting warmth shining upon us. I would not change one single moment! You have taught me that marriage and love are not stagnant destinations, but rather the celebration of love's ever-unfolding journey of life together. With your love, your compassion, and your commitment to help me heal the way I wanted to—not the way others expected me to—I became whole again. You are the rose of my life; your love and commitment shatter my fears and guide me to believe in myself once more. Thank you for always standing by me, for loving me as I Am, for unclipping my wings and allowing me to soar.

Irma Perrin: My friend, my teacher, and mentor, your inspiration and your faith in me allowed me to reflect and understand the true power within myself. You are love, peace, and all things *in spirit*; your guidance fed my soul. I am who I am today because of your love and support. Forever you are in my heart and soul.

Pamela MacEachern: It took me many years to find you. You are a friend of my heart, my soul, and I am truly blessed we found each other at long last. You are a part of me, as I am you. Together we have shared our dreams, our goals, our happiness, and laughter, as well as our sorrows and tears. You have seen me stand in triumph when I was strong and bold; you have seen me in my weakest state when I crumbled and did not want to go on. You have listened to the pain within my soul as I have yours and, through it all, I have known that what we share goes beyond the words I could use to describe this friendship. We stand together protecting the other and share unconditional love and support. I love you now and forever. We are soul mates, eternal friends, thank you for your love and friendship.

Diane Harrison: We are proof that friendships can blossom even though we have never met! I am truly blessed to know you, as we chat on cyber space. We have shared our laughter, our determination to "live life well" no matter our diseases. Thank you for being my eyes and my brain as my first practice editor. Through the numerous corrections from spelling, wrong words, and even made-up words in my work, I learned from you to have patience with myself. Also, you reminded me to be proud of the work I had written, no matter that my brain at times failed me. Thank you for your guidance, support, everlasting patience, and the numerous times you have read this manuscript prior to publishing.

Mary J. Hanlon: My late grandmother of St. Boswells, Scotland, You were my *All,* Granny. I miss you dreadfully and love you eternally. Though you were taken unexpectedly, I know you will sense my love and thankfulness for having had you as my grandmother. Your soul's understanding, kindness, and unconditional love taught me, and then my children, so much. To them you will always be their "Scotland Granny". You are with us always!

John A. Hanlon (Alec): My late grandfather of St. Boswells, Scotland. Your stoic and peaceful presence instilled in me the power of silent love. Your humor and sparkling eyes helped release my own laughter hidden within. I hope you found a GoldWing (touring motorcycle) to perch upon in heaven, for you surely looked like a king straddling Terry's motorcycle, smiling brightly as if you were ten. Memories I will treasure forever.

Susan Stephenson: (PSW, Red Cross, CCAC): You have been caring for me since I was released from the hospital. You always have a smile and kind word to help me through a rough day. Your homecare gave me my strength, self-esteem, and dignity back. Thank you for all you do to make it easier for me to live well with MS. You are amazing!

Eileen Mennim: We both travel through our lives with MS. But within the challenges of that journey, we have each still managed to share strength, love, compassion, and forgiveness. May the fruits of your spiritual journey bring you Divine light, peace, and happiness always. You have been nourishment for my soul, and I am truly blessed and eternally grateful for your friendship. Thank you for your love, support, and the many prayers you have sent my way.

Monique MacEachern: On our journey through this life, we meet many tender souls. You are one of those souls and have touched me deeply. You have a healing wisdom far beyond what my words could describe. Thank you for your guiding love and support.

Bill Stansel: You have continued to help us in any way needed. Your love and support truly helped me to take time to heal, and to see beyond my own boundaries with MS. I am not sure how I can ever thank you enough, except to tell you that your love and support gave me strength. Thank you for all you do around our home to keep up the maintenance, knowing it drove me nuts not being able to do it myself. We love you!

Mrs. Judy Bolzan & Ms. Sarah Bolzan: For the many times you both stepped forwards to help us as a family. You both understood my new difficulties with language and gave freely of your time and efforts to help Alastair succeed in his academics, especially his reading. ~ Mrs. Bolzan, thank you for giving me a chance to visit your classroom and read some of my writing. It was the first time after diagnosis that I felt I could still contribute and have meaning in my life. It was an amazing experience that energized my soul!

St Paul's School Staff, especially Mrs. GM: For all the extra support and attention you gave all our children to help them succeed. You were all very compassionate and understanding of the difficulties we faced as a family dealing with MS. But more important, you all helped our children through the stressful times to discover their own ability to succeed. You all stepped up to help us, knowing our children were facing multiple challenges at such very young ages, not only within themselves, but also in the family. From our hearts and souls, we thank you. You helped us find some strength and hope once again.

Mrs. Veld: For reaching out to Courtney when she needed it the most. I can never thank you enough for your act of kindness. To a student there is always one teacher that stands apart from the rest. One that no matter how many years go by, they are always fresh within their mind. To Courtney you are that teacher!

Marion & John De Gray: You have both inspired me with your carefree love of life. Your laughter and love was a much needed reprieve from the challenges I faced daily. When I needed someone who could help me keep my inner light glowing, you were both there. Thank you, too, for your love and friendship, for sharing fun times with Terry and our children where they did not have to think of MS. ~ To Marion, for swallowing our children in warm, loving hugs that they always looked forwards to. ~ To John, for hating the mud as much as Terry loves it. (Our pictures of John tell a different story …)

Mazinaw Mudders (Gerry, John, Peter, and Terry): Thank you all for giving Terry and our children a much needed respite from the stress and challenges we faced as a family dealing with MS. It gave them the time to be carefree, to just relax and have some mud fun. ~ To Gerry, you will be sadly missed, but always loved.

MS Society, CCAC, Red Cross: For all the services you provide that help me to live well with MS.

Rita: For all your love and laughter, your kindness and compassion. You were a beacon of light on a sometimes darkened journey. Thank you for your friendship.

Denise Linn: For reaching out to me, sharing your warmth and love. For seeing the beauty of the butterfly within me, before I saw it myself.

Robert Laidlaw: Thank you for the numerous sources of entertainment that sparked my interest. For your humorous emails that made me laugh till the tears fell. For being a most excellent sparring partner when I needed it the most.

Matt Lee: For just being yourself! You have wisdom beyond your years, and your big loving hugs were healing to me all on there own. You are an incredible young man.

Our Extended Family: To all our extended family, we thank you for all your help on this difficult and challenging journey.

All the Angels who walk amongst us: I would like to thank everyone else who came forwards to help my family throughout the difficult times. The list of names is too numerous to mention; however each one of you gave compassion and love in your own way, thus helping my healing and also my family's. I am grateful more than words can say and awed at your generosity and your compassion. We all, as a family, thank you!

Turn the page for a look at

The Poetic Soul
A Journey of the Spirit through MS

Maureen Philpott Napier

Available Soon

Sacred Moments

The silence within one's soul
Brings comfort to one's heart as they go
Forth, on their journey to understanding
Thy own awakening of the bliss
Of inner faith and love
That somehow before, we missed
Step gently on sacred ground
For the grasses and flowers do grow
Their beauty's transcendent
It needs not time to show
Its beauty, its brilliance

Each morning's dew
Gently touches the grasses as they sway
And on the petal tips of roses
As we gently bring their scent to our noses
In silence and awe
We feel our inner love shine
For in this majestic, sacred moment
Our soul's awakened
Faith and love intertwined
All as one, one as all
In God's plentiful garden we do walk
For in this silence, we renewed our faith and hope
On this, our journey of our soul

Maureen Philpott Napier
September 30, 2008

His Wisdom Reflects Through Me

The words flood through my soul
I acknowledge the creativeness I do not own
His power surfaces within me
After reflections and contemplations
Thoughts where I have released my ego and time
The Divine is within me and I shine

I am sometimes unaware of the words I write
They flow as the river flows
As day offers light
As darkness comes to night
Yet as I write I feel whole and complete
Connected, a oneness to all that is around me

I am the tree
With roots so strong
I am the sea
Beautiful waves that sing their song
I am the animal
No matter its name
Our hearts beat
We each breathe
And consume food to feed

What is all around me, I Am
And what I Am is around me
We are One
Words expressed release my creative soul
His wisdom reflects through me
In the words written by the spirit I Am
That you do not see

Maureen Philpott Napier
August 24, 2007

Thy Lessons Revealed

In the clouds of forgetfulness
I sought outside of myself
Happiness, love, knowledge
Possessions, fortunes
And the richness of this world
Day after day I searched
Month after month I spent
Outside of myself, always searching
For what, sometimes I was not sure

Yet now, as I stand naked and somewhat alone
I have come to understand my own foolishness
The searching outside of myself has exhausted this body
The searching for richness to complete myself
Was at best dauntingly dark and cold
For it removed what little richness I had internally
Until one day the clouds parted
And I awoke to thy own truth

How blind I was
Yet now, I can see
The richness was already deep within me
I Am rich; I need not possessions or more materials to fill my home
I Am loved, by my own spirit that keeps me whole
Forgive my foolishness, Beloved
I have finally learned to not look outside of myself
No matter how life externally plays on this my journey
I understand my soul's truth within
I am free to be all that I Am from within

Thank you for your lessons
For what I have learned
Has set me free
To be all that I have chosen to be
Spirit, loved and whole
The richness within me lets me soar

Maureen Philpott Napier
October 1, 2008

The Full Moon

The full moon casts its magical spell
As day surrenders its light
To the darkness of the night
But, suspended high above
The cloud covered nightly sky
The full moon makes her call
And I watch, as if mesmerized by
The hauntingly blackness of the night
Yet I hear the moons battle cry
"I Am the Night, I Am darkness and I Am the Light"

Each the moon holds dear
And allows both darkness and light to merge as one
Its fullness casts what at times looks like shadows
A portal to another dimension
If only I could walk through, the separating clouds
As if the mists of clouds themselves frame the moon
With a tinge of brownish grey embellishing its full edges
I can look and understand the mischief of this moon

It boldly lets us know
That it may sleep throughout each day
Casting little, if any, light
At times, it cannot even be seen
But wait for darkness to come
And see the beauty of the full moon arising
High above the darkened sky
Knowing that in a few short hours
It shines the brightest by far
By sharing its moonlight

Upon a darkened Earth
Always powerful, always true
This it does, every single night
For you

Maureen Philpott Napier
January 11, 2009

Between the Moments I Live

There are moments within my days
When weakness permeates every cell of this body
I have not the strength; it seems, to even breathe
For within the difficulty of filling my lungs
My body screams for surrender
The fatigue, a coma I live awake
I listen not

Yet in not listening, and thus not slowing down
Do I perpetuate the chronic pain, and darkness?
Of a disease that at times has engulfed me
I battle, but who is my enemy
Disease or thoughts, perhaps even both
And I wonder; how can the cells within this body
Live well, with peace, love and forgiveness
When each moment, in everyday, is a battle
Of surviving the pain
I am once more seeking within myself
The answers to my own inner freedom
I seek an absolute knowing within my soul
That no matter whether darkness comes from disease, or thought
There is within this soul, a spark that continues to grow
And it guides me home

Eternal peace, eternal love
The understanding that I am more than flesh and bone
As such, my soul remembers
Thy Divine vibrations of source
Where thy energy is pure
And where, all thy energy is interconnected

As Beloved's children, we are One with thee
All learning our lessons as we journey on
In His Divine company
We belong

Maureen Philpott Napier
January 8, 2009

As It Is, So Shall It Be

A new day begins
A new year is underway
That in itself, is a miracle for me
We react to what we see
What we feel
As the day passes to night
As the years pass to decades
What is
And what was
Will help determine what will be
A thought from the chatter of one's mind
Distributes the energy
Of what is to be
For me

In that understanding
I alone acknowledge my path
My choices
As it has been felt
As it has been thought
So shall it be
And so I am perplexed
At this thought of existence
One's soul, the essence of thy spirit
Eternal life, eternal energy

Yet as I contemplate these thoughts
And as they roam within this mind
I too understand the beauty of imperfection
Thy disease may cripple and change this sense of body
Yet as I let go of what I think I should be
Let go of what is perfect and what is not
Let go of what is happiness and what is not
Let go of what is beauty and what is not
I find that, even within imperfection there is beauty

Even in darkness I can see
Thy spirit is whole, for I feel it
From deep within, my soul shines
Vibrant like the storms of energy
That course through natures skies
Calm like the ripples upon the sleepy pond
Strong like the mighty oaks, I Am
Soaring like the birds flying so high
In a startling deep blue sky
I come to understand within myself
As it is, so shall it be
And the rest matters not to me

Maureen Philpott Napier
January 8, 2009

Memories of Thy Moon

Why is it that you call?
My heart and soul seemed to recall
Last month's full moon, in the nightly sky
Tonight once again, I am mesmerized
As the full moon, whispers my name
Once again, once again, once again
But it is a name, from so long ago
One I do not even recognize as my own
What is it that draws me to you?
Why is it that you call, with a silent song?
To dance with me within my mind
Thoughts drift with feelings
And I can sense
From long ago I once stood
Amongst the flowers and heavenly scents
And gazed upon thy full moons love
A different era perhaps
But always the same moon as up above
And I heard myself say
I am here once more as I lay
Amongst the field of flowers
And I prayed to you, thy full moon
With an ever increasing power
Memories of thy moon
Awake within, as I remember
The beauty of thy moon that I devour

Maureen Philpott Napier
February 8, 2009

One Moment That Is

There is a moment in one's life
When only clarity awakens thy soul
Of what was, what is, and what will be
For they will always be, where they are destined to be
What was, forever locked within thy past
What will be, forever in dreams
And our hopes that we cast
Yet what is, is always present
You cannot stand in what was and know what is
Just as you cannot stand in what will be
And thus know, what is
What is, is this special moment in life
That we acknowledge as, the *now*
I awaken to this, thy own sense
Of what *I Am,* in this moment in time
A Divine essence, a seedling planted so long ago
Continues, moment by moment, to grow
And awakens to share its compassion, its love
In the blessings of this moment that we are all a part of
The moment that is, the moment for All
Known as the Divine unity of One
With the moment that is, for it has just begun

Maureen Philpott Napier
February 1, 2009

The Butterfly

I am a little caterpillar
Wrapped up in my cocoon
But I will be a beautiful butterfly
And spread my wings soon
You will soon believe in me
As my wings set out to fly to thee

For I am strong
I am weak
And everything in between
That's what makes the colours
In my wings so vibrant and new

You will surely notice then
This butterfly has brilliance deep within
So when it's my time to explore
And leave my warm cocoon
I will stand so very tall
And fly past you, to show you all

My beautiful wings help me fly
Where I will spread my love
To all that I pass by

Maureen Philpott Napier
January 3, 2006

In the Darkness of the Night

I sit quietly
Aware of the darkness all around
Night has fallen
The darkness swallows me whole

It is a different darkness than what I am accustomed to
There are shadows or glimmers of shapes
I know not of what, but they are there all the same
They are unimportant as I scan this farmland
The darkness of this night
Is peaceful with no sight
I am before you unclothed
Masks and costumes of the day
Peel off and slip away

I am here and I am not
As the fogs moistness
Washes through me
I do not walk but somehow float
Through the gardens of Mother Nature's farms
I am one. I am whole
Somehow I realize this is the real me
I do belong
For the fog and I have become One

Maureen Philpott Napier
January 3, 2006

The Light Within

The winds of life keep changing
Affecting my light within
Seems as though these winds are affecting
My candle of light that equals my life and thus its glow

For at times my light shines brightly
Nothing, it seems, will stop me
Other times it shines so mildly
As if uncertain in its path
My candlelight flickers and falters
As these winds pick up speed, I ponder
My direction, my focus and my goals

This uncertainness seems to show
The flickering of my candlelight grows
Proving I am aware of my emotions that seem to scare
The very essence I have inside, which is I
The reflection I see is marred with scars, I cannot help but stare
The pain is the same as the high winds it seems
Threatening my life
The flickering candlelight within

Maureen Philpott Napier
December 12, 2005

Each Step I Take with Faith

As I look within
This beaten body's soul
I am as if a child newly born
All is simple, All is truth
Worries escape me
Laughter and love swallow me whole
It is in this moment of complete surrender
That I am aware of His Divine touch
On this path I walk

For there is a connection to
Something far greater than myself
In this linear time I sense
The completeness of His circle
The consciousness of All fuels my awareness
Of essence, of spirit
Yet in this life, this body has struggled to survive
Each challenge I faced, I received scars but survived
Then came the understanding that each scar was but a lesson
And now as this disease known as Multiple Sclerosis
At times takes the very breath I need to live
In this too, I am aware that though this path proves difficult
I walk it gladly

For in the steps taken I have found thy own truth
The essence of soul that is I
Remains as it has, always
Like the rivers that ever so slowly flow
Towards the oceans where their essence once came
I too, merge with the vibrational energy of source
And know I Am truly Home
Even though I walk this journey

With the ever increasing challenges I face
This journey I walk with love
Continued hope and faith
A gift from the Divine above

Maureen Philpott Napier
December 28, 2008

An Angel Is Born

There are times in your life
When you feel all alone
But don't despair for
That is the time
When Angels are born

For when their need is the greatest
That's when they arrive
Gently guiding and helping you to survive

So in those moments
When you're lost or
Your emotions seem torn
Never fear the moment
For if you
Look over your shoulder
Your Angel was born
To look after you

Maureen Philpott Napier
January 3, 2006

Love Is a Rose

They say love is like a beautiful rose
The blooms have radiance and beauty
When the fragrance reaches your nose
You can't help but breathe deeply

At times they are strong
The blossom's petals tightly closed
As the rose ages the blooms risk exposing
Their vibrant and colourful petals inside

As you gaze at its beauty
You can't help but touch
That's when you feel the thorns and get cut
They're a reminder to those
Some things are better just left and observed

The winds may pick up
Blowing petals aside
Now the beautiful bloom looks rather ragged and tired
Before long its wilted and gone

But for those that take care of the roses they own
They faithfully water and fertilize the soil
Trim and prune and spend time with
This rose bush that may look rather tired
For although the rose bush may not look that great
A gardener that takes care will have blooms again

Maureen Philpott Napier
January 5, 2006

My Love of Oceans

The oceans call to me
Salted mists I taste
As the waves, my soul they bathe
The colours crisp and new
Bring me closer to you
For in my mind I feel
The serenity and peace I crave
My soul opens up for thee
I absorb, my Lord's love He gave

Crashing waves one by one
Beauty blinding
Do others see, I wonder
The magical moment when past is gone, future untold
For nothing matters except the present as it unfolds

My life, my path, my Divine destiny
You carry within your loving plan
Beloved please guide me when you can
For now, I accept the beauty I see
As waves crash upon my heart
Renewing my spirit and soul
I send my blessings and gratitude to thee

Maureen Philpott Napier
March 5, 2006

Align Your Soul

In memories not forgotten
And pain never released
Acknowledge the thoughts
For they keep you in fear

With faith
Take the step
With trust
Know the bridge will be there

See the love
Shining from above
As Beloved held your hand
For He always understands
And He is always there
No matter the challenge
No matter the fear
Believe in the great Mystery
Of vibrations above
Align your soul
For then, inner peace
And freedom you will know
Within Beloved's wisdom and love
Life's beauty you are a part of

Maureen Philpott Napier
December 18, 2007

As Night Dawns

The sun has set
As night dawns
One ending
As one is beginning
Day to night
Night to day
The circle of life
Is much the same way

As one life ends
Another is born
And so the circle of life
Continues through time
And forever more
With each day and each night
I notice the circle is now complete

A journey begun
Comes to an end
Yearnings and learnings
Transcend the time that is now
And time has come to acknowledge
The journey completed and challenges met
Have enabled thy spirit to return home
Life's rising as the sun
Has run its course
Now thy life sets
As night dawns

Maureen Philpott Napier
September 13, 2007

Mysteries of the Divine

Comfort for thy soul
Soothe, relax and enjoy
The mysteries of the Divine
Seductively haunting
As it touches the corners of thy mind

It brings warmth
This treasure within
And the peace you've searched for all your life
For it was already *within* you
Inner faith and love
Bring forth the mysteries of the Divine above
Thy spirit rejoices
As thy soul comes alive
Full of mysteries of the Divine

Maureen Philpott Napier
September 20, 2007

This Night and I

Night has fallen once again
Stars light up the darkness from above
In wonderment I continue to view
Many galaxies from afar
The universal consequence of thought
Coursing through this energy that is myself

Though the darkness consumes nightfall
Somewhere from deep within my spirit
Thy own soul beckons and it calls
The pulse of life as it twinkles like the stars above
I can feel this deep connection to
The energy that is greater than myself
United in consciousness, love, and in peace
I understand the freedom of *be-ing*
Part of His great whole and as such pull strength
To heal a wounded mind, body and soul

I seek stillness within myself and find
Accepting the power of one's soul can become
The beacon to draw fourth pain and misery
Releasing, then surprising myself, finding faith and hope
Like the North Star shining so brightly
In releasing and understanding this life's lessons
I have come to acknowledge the beauty within myself
As a Divine soul, I have searched on this my journey
And though I have had both sunlight and darkness to walk
Somehow in each I have pulled strength
And awakened to His greatest creation
Life, on this our own journey, an eternal destination
Of love and His light
As glorious as this nights stars and moonlight

Maureen Philpott Napier
October 12, 2008

Divine Renewal

As the day moves on
Darkness quietly grips the last rays
Of sunlight's face
Yet if we believe, from deep within
That sunlight's voice, may only be dimmed
But never erased
Then from up above, the twinkling of starlight
Renews our faith and thus our strength,
Renews our compassion and thus our love

As the blessings of darkness
Merge to become one
With the blessings of light
May we come to understand the power within our own souls
That each moment gives us the perfection of continuing life
No matter if brought by darkness or sunlight
For Beloved's Divine Light
Truly exists whether
It is day or night

Maureen Philpott Napier
December 27, 2008

It Is Enough

In the stillness of this moment
I Am alive
Thy spirit soars
Beyond the boundaries of time
Beyond the boundaries of a diseased body
Thy soul is complete

In the stillness of this moment
Life is simple, but pure
Each breath a miracle
Each moment a miracle
Beyond the voice of mindless chatter
Beyond the hands of time as they tick
I Am
And that is enough

Maureen Philpott Napier
December 28, 2008

The Silent Warrior

In the silence of falling tears
I risk my soul
Battles of self preservation
Disease versus thoughts
As they fight amongst themselves
I face my judgment day
As my fear escapes
With tears falling
In this silence I weep and I pray
For inner strength
As the silent warrior stands proudly
Between both disease and thought
And forgives both with love

Maureen Philpott Napier
January 9, 2009

Thy Winter's Dream

Opening to all possibilities
Creates Divine miracles
From within thy own soul
Thy winter's dream
Captivates without words
Its beauty escapes
Without my knowing thy time
For time matters not

Blankets of white
Protect thy Earth, and remind us
That even in a winter's dream
Or thy winter of one's life
There can be cascading beauty
Like a wondrous waterfall
One's eyes seem mesmerized
As thy heart overflows
With everlasting love

This is the perfection of nature's beauty
One can gaze and think to thyself
There can be nothing more beautiful
For thy breaths one takes, feel as though taken
On Heaven's ground
Yet the next snow fall we see
Where blankets of snow
Fall gently from thy sky
Once more we feel
As if beauty has touched our soul
For we live within the moment

That is shaped from within
But thy catalyst has always been
Accepting all possibilities
For thy miracle to begin

Maureen Philpott Napier
January 18, 2009